52 Weeks of Systematic Theology Workbook for Kids

An Illustrated Yearlong Collection of Fun Activities, Questions, and Stories to Grow in Faith

Welcome Aboard, Check Out This Limited-Time Free Bonus!

Ahoy, reader! Welcome to the Ahoy Publications family, and thanks for snagging a copy of this book! Since you've chosen to join us on this journey, we'd like to offer you something special.

Check out the link below for a FREE e-book filled with delightful facts about American History.

But that's not all - you'll also have access to our exclusive email list with even more free e-books and insider knowledge. Well, what are ye waiting for? Click the link below to join and set sail toward exciting adventures in American History.

Access your bonus here

https://ahoypublications.com/

Or, Scan the QR code!

TABLE OF CONTENTS

INTRODUCTION

"Systematic theology" sounds like a huge, grown-up phrase. But here is what it really means:we are going to learn the big truths God teaches in the Bible, and we are going to organize them so they make sense.

Think of it like building a strong treehouse. You don't toss boards into a pile and hope it works. You put the pieces in the right places. In this book, each week is one piece. Week by week, you'll see how God's Word fits together.

This book is made for kids ages 8 to 12, and it is also made for families who want to learn together. You can do it on your own, with a parent, with a sibling, or with a small group.

What You'll Do Each Week

Every chapter is split into two equal parts:

1) Learn (about half the chapter)

You'll read a short lesson that explains one big idea about God and His ways. The lesson will:

- ✟ Use a Bible verse for the week.
- ✟ Explain the verse in clear words.
- ✟ Tell a short story or example you can picture.
- ✟ Help you connect the truth to real life.

2) Do (about half the chapter)

Then you'll switch into workbook mode. You'll do activities that help the truth stick, such as:

- ✟ Fun questions (some easy, some "think deeper").
- ✟ Drawing and writing prompts.
- ✟ Matching, puzzles, and simple "knowledge check" pages.
- ✟ A full-page activity (like a coloring page, poster, or mini craft).

Some kids learn best by reading. Some learn best by doing. Most of us learn best by doing both.

What This Book Is NOT

This book is not a test you have to pass. It is not a "be perfect" book. It is not a book where you need fancy words.

It *is* a book that helps you know God better and love Him more.

A Note for Parents (and Other Grown-Ups)

Kids can handle big truths when we explain them clearly and kindly. Each week gives you a simple way to talk about God at home. If you want to join in, here are a few easy ideas:

- ✟ Read the Bible verse out loud together.
- ✟ Ask your child to tell the lesson back in their own words.

✟ Let them do the activities, then talk about one answer that stood out.

✟ Pray a short prayer at the end (even one or two sentences).

You don't need to be a Bible expert. You just need to show up and point your child to God's Word.

How to Use This Book

You can use this workbook in a few different ways:

Option 1:One chapter each week

This is the main plan. Do one lesson and one set of activities each week.

Option 2:Two short days each week

Day 1:Read the lesson and answer a few questions.

Day 2:Finish the activity pages and the full-page activity.

Option 3:Family night

Pick one night a week. Read the lesson, talk for a few minutes, then let kids complete the workbook pages.

No matter which option you pick, the goal is the same:learn what God says, believe it, and live it.

Supplies You May Want

You don't need much. But these can make it more fun:

✟ Pencils and erasers.

✟ Colored pencils or crayons.

✟ Markers (if your parents say yes).

✟ Scissors and glue (for a few craft-style pages).

✟ A Bible (or a Bible app).

One Last Thing Before You Begin

Each week has a Bible verse. The verse is not there just to decorate the page. It is there because God's Word is our safest guide.

If something in the lesson surprises you, that's okay. If a question makes you pause, that's okay too. Write your thoughts. Ask a parent. Pray. Keep going.

God is not hiding from you. He loves to teach His children.

Let's get started.

PART ONE
Know God

WEEK 1
Spot God's Power

"In the beginning God created the heavens and the earth." -
Genesis 1:1

BIG TRUTH: God is the powerful Creator of everything.

WARM-UP: Look around the room you're in. Pick one object: a chair, a pencil, a shoe, a phone, a blanket. Somebody made that object. Someone had an idea, used materials, and put it together.

Now look outside (or imagine it if you can't see outside right now): clouds, birds, trees, sunlight, wind. Those things are not made in a factory. They are part of creation.

Genesis 1:1 gives us a strong start. It doesn't begin with people being in charge. It doesn't begin with chance. It begins with **God**.

What Genesis 1:1 Is Saying

The verse says, ""In the beginning God created the heavens and the earth."

That means:

- **There was a beginning.** The world is not forever old. God started it.

- **God was there first.** God didn't "become" God later. God already was.

- **God created.** He didn't borrow parts from someone else. He made what did not exist before.

- **God created everything.** "Heavens and earth" is a Bible way of saying, "all of it."

If you can name it, God made it. If you can't name it yet, God still made it.

A Kid Picture That Helps

Imagine you walk into a kitchen and see warm cookies on a tray. You might not know who baked them, but you know this:**cookies don't bake themselves**.

Creation is like that, but bigger. The world shows that there is a Creator. The Bible tells us who that Creator is:**God**.

God's Power Is Not Like Human Power

People can do amazing things, but we always have limits.

- We get tired.
- We need supplies.
- We make mistakes.
- We don't know everything.

But God's power is not like that. God doesn't run out of strength. God doesn't need to "try harder." God never says, "Oops."

That doesn't mean God is far away or cold. It means He is strong enough to lead the world and care for His people at the same time.

Why This Matters to You

Sometimes kids think, "I'm small. My problems are small too, so maybe God doesn't care." But that's not true.

If God made the whole world, He is not confused by what confuses you.

- If you feel nervous about school, God is stronger than that fear.
- If you feel lonely, God sees you clearly.
- If your family is going through something hard, God is not powerless.

You may not get every answer you want right away. But Genesis 1:1 gives you a safe place to stand:**God is real, and God is powerful.**

Tiny Step to Try This Week

Once a day, pause for ten seconds and notice something God made. Then say a short sentence like:

"God, You made this. Thank You for Your power."

WORKBOOK ACTIVITIES

1) Verse Copy (Handwriting Practice)

Copy the verse carefully. Go slow and do your best.

"In the beginning God created the heavens and the earth."

Genesis 1:1

Now copy it again (one more time):

____

2) Fill-in-the-Blanks (Word Bank)

Fill in the missing words.

"In the   , God _________________ the _________________ and the _________________."

Word Bank:beginning, created, heavens, earth

3) Quick Check (Circle One)

1. Genesis 1:1 teaches that:

    A) the earth made itself
    B) God created everything
    C) people created the world first

2. God's power means:

    A) God gets tired quickly
    B) God needs help
    C) God can do what no one else can do

3. "Creator" means:

    A) someone who copies
    B) someone who makes
    C) someone who breaks

4) Spot God's Power (Creation List)

Write **five** things in creation that show God's power.

1. ________________________________

2. ________________________________

3. ________________________________

4. ________________________________

5. ________________________________

Star one that you want to thank God for today:

★ ________________________________

5) Big or Small? (Sorting Activity)

Write each word under the best label.

Words: ant, ocean, moon, pebble, elephant, raindrop, mountain, sunflower

Small:________________________________

Medium: ________________________________

Big: ________________________________

Now finish this sentence:

 "God made the small, the medium, and the big, so God can handle my

________________________________."

6) Picture It (Draw + Label)

Draw a simple picture of something God created. Add **three labels**.

My picture:(draw in the space underneath the lines)

Labels:

1. ________________________________

2. ________________________________

3. ________________________________

7) **Real-Life Moment (Prayer Practice)**

Choose one situation below and answer it.

Pick one:

I feel worried about school.

I feel left out.

I get angry fast.

Something at home feels hard.

Write one sentence about what's going on:

____

____

Now, write a short prayer (2–4 lines):

"Powerful God, You made the heavens and the earth.

Please help me with

____

____

____

Help me trust You today. Amen."

8) **Knowledge Check (One-Minute Review)**

Answer in one short sentence:

What does Genesis 1:1 teach you about God?

____

____

____

____

____

____

GOD
Made It All!
Genesis 1:1

WEEK 2
Praise God's Closeness

"Where can I go from your Spirit? Where can I flee from your presence? If I go up to the heavens, you are there; if I make my bed in the depths, you are there.?" - Psalm 139:7–8

BIG TRUTH: God is always present. He is close, and you can talk to Him anywhere.

WARM-UP: Have you ever played hide-and-seek and found the "perfect" hiding spot? Maybe behind a curtain, under a blanket, or tucked in a corner where nobody would look.

Hide-and-seek is fun because people can lose track of you.

But Psalm 139 says something different about God: you can't hide from Him. You can't go anywhere that God is not already there.

What Psalm 139:7–8 Is Saying

David (the writer of this Psalm) asks two questions:

- ✟ "Where shall I go from your Spirit?"
- ✟ "Where shall I flee from your presence?"

He is not trying to run away because he hates God. He is amazed. He is saying, "Is there any place I can go where You won't be there?" And the answer is:**No.**

Psalm 139 even gives examples. It says if David went up to the heavens, God would be there. If he went down to the deepest place, God would still be there. The highest place and the lowest place are both under God's care.

God's Closeness Is Good News

Some people feel nervous when they hear "God sees everything." But for God's children, this is meant to be comforting.

Think about it:

- ✞ If you feel lonely at school, God is with you.
- ✞ If you feel nervous before a test, God is with you.
- ✞ If you feel upset at home, God is with you.
- ✞ If you feel happy and excited, God is with you.

God's presence is not like a spotlight that is trying to embarrass you. It's more like a loving parent staying near their child in a crowded place. God is close because He cares.

"God Is Here" in Ordinary Places

Kids sometimes picture God only in "church places" like sanctuaries and Bible stories. But God is also present in ordinary places:

- ✞ At your kitchen table.
- ✞ In the car.
- ✞ In your classroom.
- ✞ On the sports field.
- ✞ In your bedroom at night.

This doesn't mean every place is safe or every choice is right. It means God is not locked into one building. He is the Lord over all the earth.

How God's Closeness Helps You Grow

When you remember God is near, it can change what you do next.

- ✞ You can pray right away instead of waiting.
- ✞ You can tell the truth because God is with you.
- ✞ You can ask for help when you feel stuck.
- ✞ You can choose kindness because you are never alone.

Here is a simple sentence you can use anytime: "God, You are here with me."

Tiny Step to Try This Week

Pick one moment each day (morning, lunch, or bedtime). Pause and whisper: *"God, thank You for being near."*

WORKBOOK ACTIVITIES

1) Verse Copy (Handwriting Practice)

Copy the Bible focus verse carefully:

"Where can I go from your Spirit? Where can I flee from your presence?" - **Psalm 139:7**

Copy one more time:

____

____

____

____

2) True or False

Circle **True** or **False**.

1. God is only close when I feel happy.   **True / False**
2. God is with me at school.   **True / False**
3. I can go somewhere God cannot see.   **True / False**
4. God's closeness is meant to help me.   **True / False**

3) Finish the Sentences

Fill in the blanks with your own words.

✞ God is close when I am ______________________________

✞ God is close when I feel _____________________________

✞ God is close when I need _____________________________

4) "God Is Here" Places

Write **six** places where you go in a normal week. Then write "God is here" beside each one.

1. ____ - God is here

2. ____ - God is here

3. ____ - God is here

4. ____ - God is here

5. ____ - God is here

6. ____ - God is here

5) Feelings Check-In

Have a look at the list of trust below our list of feelings. Which truths do you think we can match with each feeling? Write down the letters next to each word:

Feelings:

✟ lonely

✟ nervous

✟ angry

✟ excited

✟ ashamed

Truths:

A) God is still with me and can calm my heart.

B) God is still with me and can help me choose what's right.

C) God is still with me and can guide my next step.

D) God is still with me and I can talk to Him.

E) God is still with me and forgives those who come to Him.

   (You can use a truth more than once.)

6) Scenario Choices (Circle the Best Answer)

1. You feel left out at recess. What can you do first?

    A) Give up and sit alone forever

    B) Pray and ask God for courage

    C) Pretend you don't care and be rude

2. You're worried about a homework assignment.

    A) Ask God for help, then do your best

    B) Hide it and hope it disappears

    C) Blame someone else

3. You said something unkind and now you feel bad.

    A) Talk to God and ask forgiveness, then make it right

    B) Say, "It doesn't matter"

    C) Do it again so you feel "strong"

7) Short Prayer Practice

Write a 3–5 line prayer.

"God, thank You for being close to me.

Please help me with

____

____

Help me remember You are here at

____

____

Amen."

8) Knowledge Check (One-Minute Review)

Answer in one short sentence:

What does Psalm 139 teach you about God?

____

____

God Is With Me Everywhere!

(Psalm 139:7–8)

Find and circle each 'God is here' icon.
Color the scene when you're done.

WEEK 3
Cheer God's Greatness

"Do you not know? Have you not heard? The Lord is the everlasting God, the Creator of the ends of the earth. He will not grow tired or weary, and his understanding no one can fathom." - Isaiah 40:28

BIG TRUTH: God is everlasting, never runs out of strength, and is wiser than we can measure.

WARM-UP: Think about the biggest thing you've ever seen in real life. Maybe it was a mountain, a huge building, the ocean, or a stadium full of people. Big things can make you feel small.

Isaiah 40 talks about Someone even greater than that. It tells us what God is like.

What Isaiah 40:28 Is Saying

This verse teaches several true things about God:

✝ **"The LORD is the everlasting God."**

God does not "start" and "stop." He does not grow old. He does not fade away. God always has been God, and He always will be.

✝ **"The Creator of the ends of the earth."**

God didn't just create your town or your country. He made every place on earth. No corner is too far for Him.

✝ **"He does not faint or grow weary."**

God does not get tired the way people do. He doesn't need a nap, a snack, or a break.

✟ **"His understanding is unsearchable."**

God is wise in a way we can't fully reach. You can learn real things about God, but you'll never get to the end of His wisdom.

A Kid Picture That Helps

Have you ever played a game where you ran out of energy first? Your legs got tired, or you started breathing hard, and you had to stop.

People run out of energy. Even the strongest athletes do.

But God never runs out. God never says, "I can't handle this today." God never says, "I didn't think of that."

Why God's Greatness Is Good News

Sometimes "greatness" sounds scary, like a boss who doesn't care. But God's greatness is different.

God is great *and* good.

That means:

✟ When you have a big problem, God is not too small to help.

✟ When you have a confusing question, God is not puzzled.

✟ When you feel worn out, God is not worn out.

Here is something important: God's greatness does not push you away. It means you can trust Him more.

When You Feel Small

Kids feel small in lots of ways:

✟ someone else is taller, louder, or faster

✟ a friend group changes

✟ a test feels hard

✟ family problems feel too big

When you feel that way, Isaiah 40:28 gives you a steady truth:

God is greater than what feels big to you.

Tiny Step to Try This Week

Once a day, say this out loud: "God, You are everlasting. You are wise. You are strong."

WORKBOOK ACTIVITIES

1) Verse Copy (Handwriting Practice)

Copy the Bible focus phrase:

""Do you not know? Have you not heard? The Lord is the everlasting God, the Creator of the ends of the earth. He will not grow tired or weary, and his understanding no one can fathom."

- Isaiah 40:28

Copy it one more time:

____

____

____

____

2) Word Helper (Match the Meaning)

Draw a line to match each word to its meaning.

1. Everlasting	A) makes something
2. Creator	B) never ends
3. Weary	C) very tired
4. Understanding	D) wisdom and knowledge

3) Circle the Best Answer

1. God gets tired:

    A) often

    B) sometimes

    C) never

2. God's wisdom:

    A) has limits

    B) can't be measured fully

    C) is the same as mine

3. God is Creator of:

    A) my street only

    B) my country only

    C) the ends of the earth

4) Big vs. Small (Write It Out)

Write one thing that feels big to you right now:

____

Now write a truth from Isaiah 40:28 that helps:

____

____

Finish the sentence:

"Even when ____

feels big, God is ________________________________."

5) Strength Swap (Practice Turning to God)

Read each moment. Write what you can do next.

1. "I feel nervous before a test."

    I can: ____

2. "I feel left out."

    I can: ____

3. "I'm tired and want to give up."

I can: ____

6) **Praise List (Quick Praise)**

Write **five** praise words that fit God's greatness.

1. ____

2. ____

3. ____

4. ____

5. ____

Now write one sentence praise:

"God, You are ______________________________ and I praise You."

7) **Draw ItGod's Great World**

Draw one "big" part of creation (mountain, ocean, night sky, big tree). Then write a caption under it:

"God is greater than ______________________________________

______________________________________ ."

8) **Knowledge Check (One-Minute Review)**

Answer in one short sentence:

What does Isaiah 40:28 teach you about God?

____

____

____

God Is Greater Than All!

Isaiah 40:28

But God is everlasting and wise.

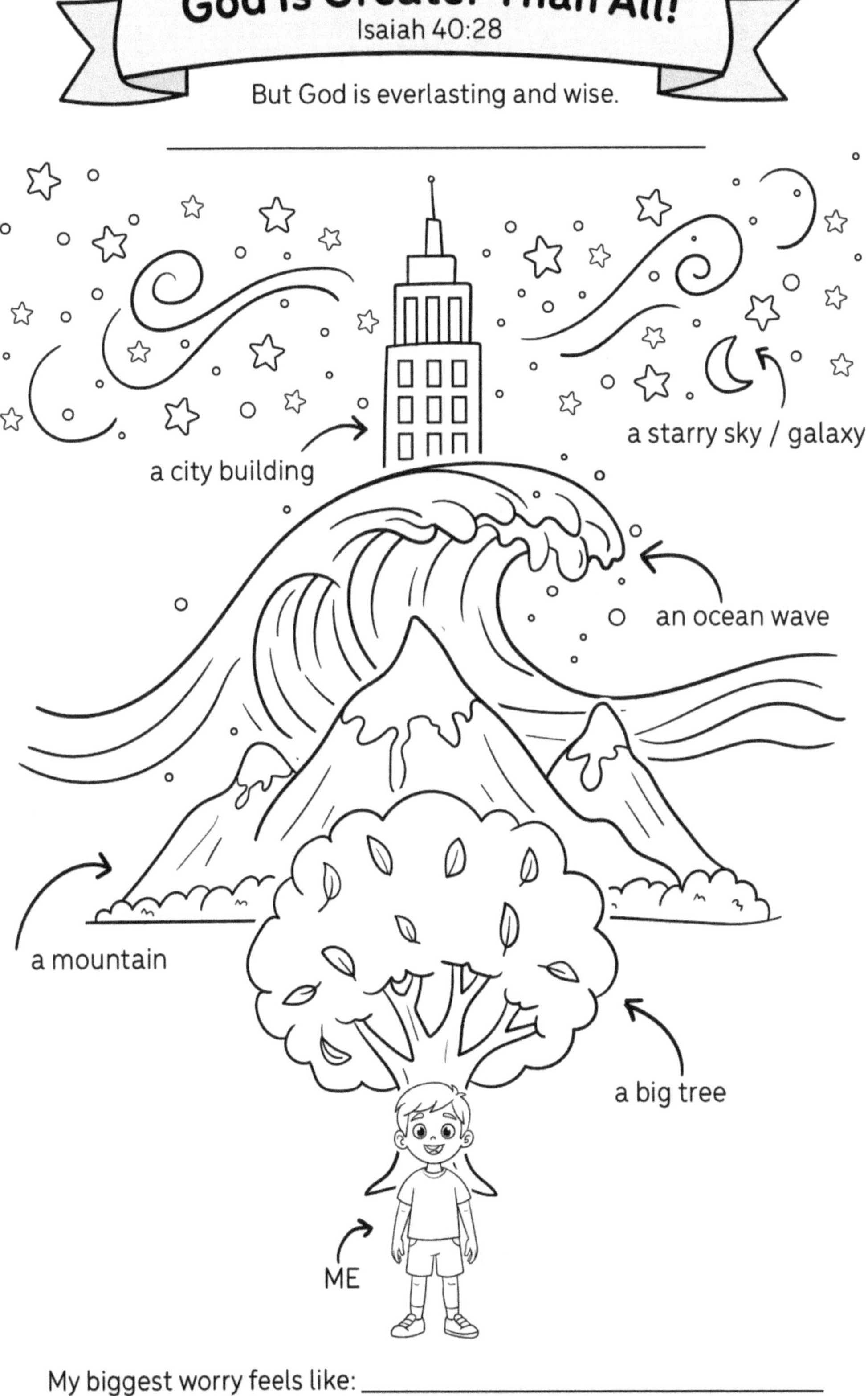

My biggest worry feels like: _______________________

WEEK 4
Love God's Kindness

"And he passed in front of Moses, proclaiming, "The Lord, the Lord, the compassionate and gracious God, slow to anger, abounding in love and faithfulness," - Exodus 34:6

BIG TRUTH: God is kind, patient, and full of faithful love.

WARM-UP: Think about the kindest thing someone has done for you. Maybe a friend shared. Maybe a teacher helped you understand something. Maybe someone forgave you when you messed up.

Kindness feels like a safe place.

Now here's an even better truth: God's kindness isn't just something He does sometimes. **God's kindness is part of who He is.**

What Exodus 34:6 Is Saying

This verse is one of the clearest "God descriptions" in the Bible. God tells us what He is like:

- ✞ **Merciful** - God shows compassion when people are in trouble.
- ✞ **Gracious** - God gives good gifts that we did not earn.
- ✞ **Slow to anger** - God is patient. He does not explode in a moment.
- ✞ **Abounding in steadfast love** - God has a lot of faithful love, and it doesn't quit.

The words "steadfast love" matter a lot. Steadfast means steady and strong. God's love doesn't wobble like a shaky chair. It stays firm.

God's Kindness Is Not Weak

Some people think kindness means you let everyone walk over you.

That's not true.

God is kind, and God is also holy. He loves what is right. He hates what is evil. But even when God corrects His people, He does it as a good Father who loves them.

God's kindness doesn't mean sin is no big deal. It means God is ready to forgive and help people who come to Him.

When You Mess Up

Kids mess up. Grown-ups mess up too. Sometimes we:

- ✝ say something mean
- ✝ tell a lie
- ✝ hide what we did
- ✝ blame someone else
- ✝ get angry fast

When that happens, you might think, "God must be tired of me."

But Exodus 34:6 says God is **slow to anger** and full of steadfast love. That means you should run *to* God, not away from Him.

A kind God invites you to confess, ask forgiveness, and start fresh.

God's Kindness Changes How We Treat People

When you know God is kind, it helps you become kind too. You start noticing people who feel left out. You stop enjoying someone else's embarrassment. You care about doing what is good.

Kindness doesn't always feel easy. But God can help you practice it.

Tiny Step to Try This Week

Choose one kindness action every day. Keep it simple:

- ✝ help without being asked
- ✝ use gentle words
- ✝ include someone
- ✝ forgive quickly

Then pray: "God, thank You for Your kindness. Help me show it too."

WORKBOOK ACTIVITIES

1) Verse Copy (Handwriting Practice)

Copy the Bible focus phrase:

"And he passed in front of Moses, proclaiming, "The Lord, the Lord, the compassionate and gracious God, slow to anger, abounding in love and faithfulness,"

Exodus 34:6

Copy it one more time:

____

____

____

2) Match the Meaning

Draw a line to match each word to its meaning.

1. Merciful		A) patient, not quick to blow up
2. Gracious		B) steady, faithful love
3. Slow to anger		C) gives good gifts we don't earn
4. Steadfast love		D) shows compassion when we fail

3) Kind or Not Kind? (Circle the Kind Choice)

1. Someone drops their pencil.

    A) laugh

    B) help pick it up

2. A friend makes a mistake reading out loud.

    A) tease them

    B) encourage them

3. You feel mad at your sibling.

    A) yell and slam doors

    B) use calm words and ask for help

4. Someone sits alone at lunch.

    A) ignore them

    B) invite them over

4) My Kindness Plan

Write two kindness actions you will do this week:

1. I will

____

____

2. I will

____

____

Now write one person you want to show kindness to:

____

____

____

____

____

5) "Slow to Anger" Practice

Read each moment. Write one patient choice.

1. "I didn't get my way."

    Patient choice:

____

____

2. "Someone annoyed me."

> Patient choice

____

____

3. "I feel like shouting."

> Patient choice

____

____

6) Steadfast Love Reminder

Finish the sentence in your own words:

God's love is steadfast, which means

____

____

____

7) Prayer Practice

Write a short prayer (4–6 lines):

"Kind God, thank You for Your steadfast love.

 Please forgive me for

____

____

____

Help me be kind to

____

____

Help me be slow to anger today. Amen."

Knowledge Check (One-Minute Review)

Answer in one short sentence:

What does Exodus 34:6 teach you about God?

God's Kindness.
share
help
encourage someone
forgive
include
gentle words
patience
honesty
friend smiling
task finished
feeling brave
friendship restored
group together
calm faces
waiting calmly
trust restored
• Color the hearts.
• Draw lines to match each kind action to what it helps.

WEEK 5
Trust God's Father Heart

"As a father has compassion on his children, so the Lord has compassion on those who fear him;" - Psalm 103:13

BIG TRUTH: God cares for His children with compassion, like a perfect Father.

WARM-UP: When you scrape your knee or feel sick, you probably want help from someone who cares. A good parent doesn't say, "Stop bothering me." A good parent gets close, helps you, and wants you to be okay.

Psalm 103:13 tells us God is like that, only better. God has **compassion** for His children.

Compassion is more than noticing. Compassion means you care deeply and you choose to help.

What Psalm 103:13 Is Saying

The verse says: "As a father has compassion on his children, ..."

That means God is not cold. He is not far away. He is not annoyed by you.

God sees His children clearly. He knows when they're hurting, nervous, confused, or ashamed. And He cares.

The verse also says "to those who fear him." In the Bible, "fear" often means respect and trust. It's not the fear of a kid being scared of a bully. It's the respect of a kid who knows a parent is wise, strong, and good.

Important Note for Kids

Not every kid's family looks the same. Some dads are loving and present. Some are absent. Some make mistakes that hurt others.

So, when the Bible uses the word "father" for God, it's not saying every human dad is perfect. It's showing us what a **perfect Father** is like.

God always does what is right. God always tells the truth. God doesn't forget you. God doesn't stop caring when you have a bad day.

God's Compassion Looks Like This

Here are some ways God's compassion shows up:

- ✟ God listens when you pray.
- ✟ God corrects you because He loves you, not because He hates you.
- ✟ God forgives when you confess your sin.
- ✟ God comforts you when you're sad.
- ✟ God gives you what you need, even when you don't understand everything.

God's compassion doesn't mean life will always feel easy. But it does mean you are never alone in life.

How Trust Grows

Trust doesn't appear overnight. Trust grows little by little.

You trust God more when you:

- ✟ read His Word
- ✟ tell Him the truth in prayer
- ✟ remember what He has done
- ✟ obey Him in small things

When you feel afraid or uncertain, you can remind yourself: **God's heart is compassionate.**

Tiny Step to Try This Week

At bedtime, say this short prayer: "Father God, thank You for caring about me. Help me trust You tomorrow too."

1) Verse Copy (Handwriting Practice)

Copy the Bible focus verse:

"As a father has compassion on his children, so the Lord has compassion on those who fear him;"

Psalm 103:13

Copy it one more time:

____

____

____

____

2) What Does Compassion Mean? (Circle One)

Compassion means:

      A) not caring

      B) caring deeply and helping

      C) pretending everything is fine

3) God's Father Heart (Fill in the Blanks)

Complete each sentence:

1. God is _______________________________ when I am hurting.

2. God _______________________________ when I pray.

3. God's care is _______________________________

    and _______________________________ .

(Use your own words.)

4) "God Cares" List

Write **five** ways God cares for His children.

1. ____

2. ____

3. ____

4. ____

5. ____

Put a star next to the one you need most today: ★

5) When I Feel… God Can…

Match the feeling to what God can do. Write the letters from the God Can sections that you feel are the best match.

Feelings:

1. nervous

2. sad

3. guilty

4. lonely

5. angry

God can:

A) forgive and help me make it right

B) comfort me

C) guide me

D) help me calm down

E) stay near me

6) Trust Steps (Choose One)

Pick **one** situation and write a "trust step."

I'm worried about school.

I'm worried about a friendship.

I'm worried about something at home.

I'm worried about my own behavior.

My situation:

____

My trust step (one thing I will do with God's help):

____

7) Dear God Letter (Writing Practice)

Write a short letter to God (6–10 lines).

Include:

- ✝ one thing you feel
- ✝ one thing you need
- ✝ one thank you

Dear God,

____

____

____

____

____

Amen.

8) Knowledge Check (One-Minute Review)

Answer in one short sentence:

What does Psalm 103:13 teach you about God?

____

____

____

____

5 Ways God Cares for Me
1.
2.
3.
4.
5.
Today I will trust God with:
God Shows Compassion — Psalm 103:13

WEEK 6
Stand on God's Truth

"God is not human, that he should lie, not a human being, that he should change his mind. Does he speak and then not act? Does he promise and not fulfill?" - Numbers 23:19

BIG TRUTH: God always tells the truth, and God always keeps His promises.

WARM-UP: Have you ever had someone promise something and then not do it?

Maybe they said, "I'll be there," and they didn't show up. Maybe they said, "I'll help you," and they forgot. Maybe they said, "I won't tell," and then they told.

People don't always keep their word. Sometimes it's on purpose. Sometimes it's because they are weak, distracted, or selfish.

But Numbers 23:19 teaches a steady truth:**God is different.**

What Numbers 23:19 Is Saying

The verse begins:"God is not man, that he should lie..."

That means:

  ✝ God does not lie like people can.

  ✝ God does not "stretch" the truth.

  ✝ God does not pretend.

  ✝ God does not make fake promises.

The verse goes on to show that God does what He says. If God speaks, it is true. If God promises, He keeps it.

Why This Matters

Truth is like solid ground. When you know what is true, you can make wise choices.

But lies are like slippery ice. They make everything shaky. Lies can:

- hurt friendships
- break trust
- create fear
- make problems bigger

God's truth does the opposite. God's truth:

- builds trust
- brings light
- helps you know what is right
- gives courage when you feel afraid

God's Truth Helps You Know Who to Trust

Sometimes you hear lots of voices:

- friends
- social media
- movies
- your own feelings
- your own fears

Some voices are helpful. Some are not. Some are wrong.

So where do you go when you want truth that won't change? You go to God's Word.

God's Word is not a guessing game. It is a guide. When you read the Bible, you learn what God says is true about:

- who God is
- who you are

✞ what sin is

✞ what salvation is

✞ what wise living looks like

Truth and Feelings

Feelings can be real, but feelings are not always right.

You might *feel* like nobody cares, but God's truth says He does. You might *feel* like you can't change, but God's truth says He helps His children grow. You might *feel* like you should hide, but God's truth calls you to come into the light.

Truth doesn't crush you. Truth helps you.

Tiny Step to Try This Week

When you feel confused, say: "God, show me what is true."

Then read a Bible verse, talk to a trusted adult, and take one right step.

WORKBOOK ACTIVITIES

1) Verse Copy (Handwriting Practice)

Copy the Bible focus phrase:

"God is not human, that he should lie, not a human being, that he should change his mind. Does he speak and then not act? Does he promise and not fulfill?" - **Numbers 23:19**

Copy it one more time:

____

____

____

____

2) **Fill in the Blank**

"God is not man, that he should ________________________________

____."

(Write the missing word.)

3) **True or False**

Circle **True** or **False**.

1. God sometimes lies.   **True / False**

2. God keeps His Word.   **True / False**

3. God's promises can be trusted.   **True / False**

4. God changes His mind about loving His children.   **True / False**

4) **Truth or Trick? (Mark T or X)**

Write **T** if it matches God's truth. Write **X** if it does not.

1. ________ "God loves His children."

2. ________ "God wants me to lie if it helps me."

3. ________ "God forgives those who confess and turn back to Him."

4. ________ "God doesn't care what I do when no one is watching."

5. ________ "God is with me even when I feel alone."

6. ________ "God says it's fine to be cruel if I'm upset."

5) **Choose the Truth (Circle One)**

1. You broke something and feel scared.

    A) Hide it and blame someone else

    B) Tell the truth and ask for help

2. Your friend is gossiping about someone.

    A) Join in so you fit in

    B) Stop and choose words that are right

3. You feel like quitting something hard.

    A) Give up instantly

    B) Ask God for strength and keep going

6) Truth for My Life (Write It)

Write one situation where you need truth right now:

____

____

Now write one truthful sentence you can remember:

____

____

Finish this sentence:

"When I feel _________________________________ ,

I will stand on God's truth by _________________ ."

7) Build Trust (Short Reflection)

Answer in 2–3 sentences:

Why is it important that God does not lie?

____

____

____

____

8) Prayer Practice

Write a prayer (4–7 lines):

"True God, thank You that You never lie.

Please help me tell the truth about

____

____

____

____

____

Help me trust Your promises when I feel

____

____

____

____

Help me choose what is right today. Amen."

9) Knowledge Check (One-Minute Review)

Answer in one short sentence:

What does Numbers 23:19 teach you about God?

____

____

____

____

____

____

____

____

____

____

____

____

____

____

Stand on God's Truth — Numbers 23:19

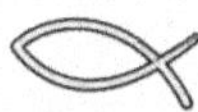

Circle the bubbles that match God's truth."

One truth I want to remember this week: ______________________

____

PART TWO
God's Word

WEEK 7
Hold Tight to Scripture

"All Scripture is God-breathed and is useful for teaching, rebuking, correcting and training in righteousness," - 2 Timothy 3:16

BIG TRUTH: The Bible is God's Word, and it helps you know what is true and how to live.

WARM-UP: Imagine you're trying to build something awesome, like a LEGO set, but you refuse to use the instructions. You might still build something, but it probably won't look right, and it will take longer. You may even end up frustrated.

Life can feel like that too. You can try to figure everything out on your own, but God didn't leave you without help. He gave you the Bible.

What 2 Timothy 3:16 Is Saying

This verse tells us something huge: **"All Scripture is breathed out by God."**

That doesn't mean God literally breathed on paper like fog on a window. It means the Bible comes from God. God used real people to write it, in real places and times, but the message is God's message. So when you read Scripture, you are not just reading human opinions. You are hearing God's truth.

Then the verse says Scripture is "profitable," which means **useful**. It helps you in real ways:

- ✝ **Teaching** - It shows you what is true about God, sin, salvation, and life.
- ✝ **Reproof** - It helps you notice what is wrong. (Like a warning sign.)

57

✝ **Correction** - It helps you get back on the right path.

✝ **Training in righteousness** - It helps you practice living God's way.

The Bible is not a decoration. It's a tool God uses to shape your heart.

The Bible Helps You in Everyday Life

Sometimes kids think the Bible is only for adults or pastors. But Scripture is for you too.

The Bible can help you:

✝ know God better

✝ choose honesty when lying feels easier

✝ forgive when you want revenge

✝ feel hope when you feel afraid

✝ learn what love looks like

Even one verse can help you take one wise step.

"All Scripture" Means All of It

"All Scripture" doesn't mean only the easy parts or the favorite parts. It means the whole Bible is God's Word.

Some parts are stories. Some are songs. Some are letters. Some parts explain laws or give warnings. You won't understand everything at once, and that's okay. The goal is not to rush. The goal is to keep learning with a humble heart.

How to Hold Tight to Scripture

Holding tight doesn't mean squeezing the Bible like a stress ball. It means:

✝ reading it

✝ listening carefully

✝ believing what God says is true

✝ obeying it, even in small ways

Here's a simple idea:when you read a verse, ask:

1. What does this teach me about God?

2. What does this show me about how to live?

Tiny Step to Try This Week

Pick one short verse from this chapter's activities. Read it every day for seven days. Try to say it without looking by the end of the week.

WORKBOOK ACTIVITIES

1) **Verse Copy (Handwriting Practice)**

Copy the Bible focus verse carefully:

"All Scripture is God-breathed and is useful for teaching, rebuking, correcting and training in righteousness," **2 Timothy 3:16**

Copy one more time:

____

____

____

____

____

____

____

2) **Bible Word Match**

Draw a line to match each word to its meaning.

1. Scripture   A) helpful and good for you

2. Profitable   B) God's written Word (the Bible)

3. Teaching   C) showing what is true

4. Correction   D) helping you get back on track

5. Training   E) practice that makes you stronger

3) **Quick Check (Circle One)**

1. The Bible is:

    A) just old stories

    B) people's best guesses

    C) God's Word

2. "Breathed out by God" means:

    A) God sneezed on pages

    B) the message comes from God

    C) the Bible is only for adults

3. Scripture helps with:

    A) teaching only

    B) teaching, reproof, correction, and training

    C) nothing important

4) **Spot the Bible's Help**

Write one example for each:

Teaching (what is true):

____

____

____

Reproof (what is wrong):

____

____

Correction (how to fix it):

____

____

Training (how to practice):

____

____

5) **Real-Life Situations**

Read each situation. Write one way Scripture could help.

1. You're tempted to lie to avoid trouble.

    Scripture helps me by:

    ____

    ____

2. You feel worried at night.

    Scripture helps me by:

    ____

    ____

3. You're mad at a friend.

    Scripture helps me by

    ____

    ____

4. You feel left out.

    Scripture helps me by

    ____

    ____

6) **My "Hold Tight" Plan**

Circle one plan you will try this week:

      A) Read one Bible verse each day

      B) Ask a grown-up to read the Bible with me twice this week

      C) Memorize one short verse

      D) Write one verse on a card and keep it near my bed

Write your plan here:

____

____

____

____

____

7) Short Prayer Practice

Write a prayer (4–7 lines):

"God, thank You for giving me Scripture.

____

____

Please teach me what is true.

____

____

Show me when I am wrong, and help me change.

____

____

Train my heart to love what is right

____

____

Amen."

8) Knowledge Check (One-Minute Review)

Answer in one short sentence:

What does 2 Timothy 3:16 teach you about the Bible?

____

____

____

____

____

God's Word Helps Me!
2 Timothy 3:16
Teaching
Reproof
Correction
Training

WEEK 8
Listen When God Speaks

"For the word of God is alive and active. Sharper than any double-edged sword, it penetrates even to dividing soul and spirit, joints and marrow; it judges the thoughts and attitudes of the heart." - Hebrews 4:12

BIG TRUTH: God uses His Word to speak to you, guide you, and show what's really going on in your heart.

WARM-UP: Have you ever heard your name called in a noisy place? Maybe at a store, at school, or on a playground. Lots of voices are happening, but when someone says your name, you notice.

God speaks in a way that matters even more than that. He speaks through **His Word**, the Bible.

Hebrews 4:12 tells us something surprising: God's Word isn't like a dusty old book that sits on a shelf. God's Word is **living and active**.

What "Living and Active" Means

When something is living, it has real life. When something is active, it does real work.

The Bible is "living and active" because God uses it right now, today, to help His people. When you read Scripture, God can:

- ✝ comfort you
- ✝ correct you
- ✝ warn you
- ✝ encourage you
- ✝ teach you
- ✝ strengthen your faith

Sometimes you read a verse you've heard before, but this time it hits your heart in a new way. That is God's Word at work.

God's Word Helps You Tell What's True

Hebrews 4:12 also says God's Word can "discern the thoughts and intentions of the heart."

That means Scripture helps you see what's happening inside you.

For example:

- ✟ You might say, "I'm just joking," but your heart might be trying to hurt someone.
- ✟ You might say, "I don't care," but your heart might be afraid of being rejected.
- ✟ You might say, "It's fine," but your heart might be holding a grudge.

God's Word doesn't do this to shame you. God does it to help you. When you know what is in your heart, you can confess sin, ask for help, and choose what is right.

Listening Is a Skill

Listening to God doesn't mean you wait for a voice in your ear. For most people, listening to God looks like this:

- ✟ you read the Bible
- ✟ you pay attention
- ✟ you ask God to teach you
- ✟ you obey what you understand

Sometimes kids ask, "What if I don't understand the Bible?" That's normal. Some parts are hard. But you can still listen. Start with small pieces. Ask a trusted adult. Read the verse again slowly. God loves to help His children learn.

A Helpful Question (And the Answer)

"How do I know if a thought in my head is from God?"

A good way is to compare it to Scripture.

✝ If the thought says, "Lie to stay out of trouble," that does not match God's Word.

✝ If the thought says, "Tell the truth and ask forgiveness," that matches God's Word.

✝ If the thought says, "Get revenge," that does not match God's Word.

✝ If the thought says, "Forgive and make peace," that matches God's Word.

God's Word helps you sort thoughts like a filter.

Tiny Step to Try This Week

Before you read Scripture this week, pray this short prayer:

"God, please speak to me through Your Word. Help me listen and obey."

WORKBOOK ACTIVITIES

1) Verse Copy (Handwriting Practice)

Copy the Bible focus phrase:

"For the word of God is alive and active. Sharper than any double-edged sword, it penetrates even to dividing soul and spirit, joints and marrow; it judges the thoughts and attitudes of the heart." - **Hebrews 4:12**

Copy it one more time:

____

____

____

____

2) Finish the Statement

Fill in the blanks:

The Word of God is _______________________________________

and ____ .

(Use the words from the verse.)

3) True or False

Circle **True** or **False**.

1. The Bible is only for people long ago.   **True / False**

2. God can use Scripture to guide me today.   **True / False**

3. God's Word can help me see what's in my heart.   **True / False**

4. Listening to God means I never have questions.   **True / False**

4) Heart Check (Thoughts and Intentions)

Circle the best answer.

1. "Intentions" are:

    A) what you eat for lunch

    B) the reasons behind what you do

    C) how fast you can run

2. God's Word helps with:

    A) hiding what's in your heart

    B) showing what's in your heart

    C) making you proud

5) Sort the Thoughts (Write S for Scripture / N for Not Scripture)

Write **S** if the thought matches God's Word. Write **N** if it does not.

1. __________ "I should forgive when someone says sorry."

2. __________ "If I'm mad, I should hurt them back."

3. __________ "I should tell the truth, even when it's hard."

4. __________ "God won't care if I'm mean online."

5. __________ "I can ask God for help when I'm scared."

6. __________ "It's fine to cheat as long as no one sees."

6) Listening Practice (3 Steps)

Write one sentence for each step:

1. When I read the Bible, I will listen to _______________________
2. God might be showing me to change _______________________
3. One way I can obey this week is _______________________

7) Short Scenario Choose the Right Path

Pick one scenario and answer both questions.

Scenario A: You want to fit in, so you feel pressure to laugh at someone.

✝ What does my heart want?

____

____

✝ What does God's Word teach?

____

____

Scenario B: You did something wrong and want to hide it.

✝ What does my heart want?

____

____

____

✝ What does God's Word teach?

____

____

____

8) Prayer Practice

Write a prayer (4–7 lines):

"God, thank You that Your Word is living and active.

____

____

____

Please show me what is in my heart.

____

____

____

Help me turn from sin and choose what is right.

____

____

____

Help me obey You this week.

Amen."

9) Knowledge Check (One-Minute Review)

Answer in one short sentence:

What does Hebrews 4:12 teach you about God's Word?

____

____

____

____

____

____

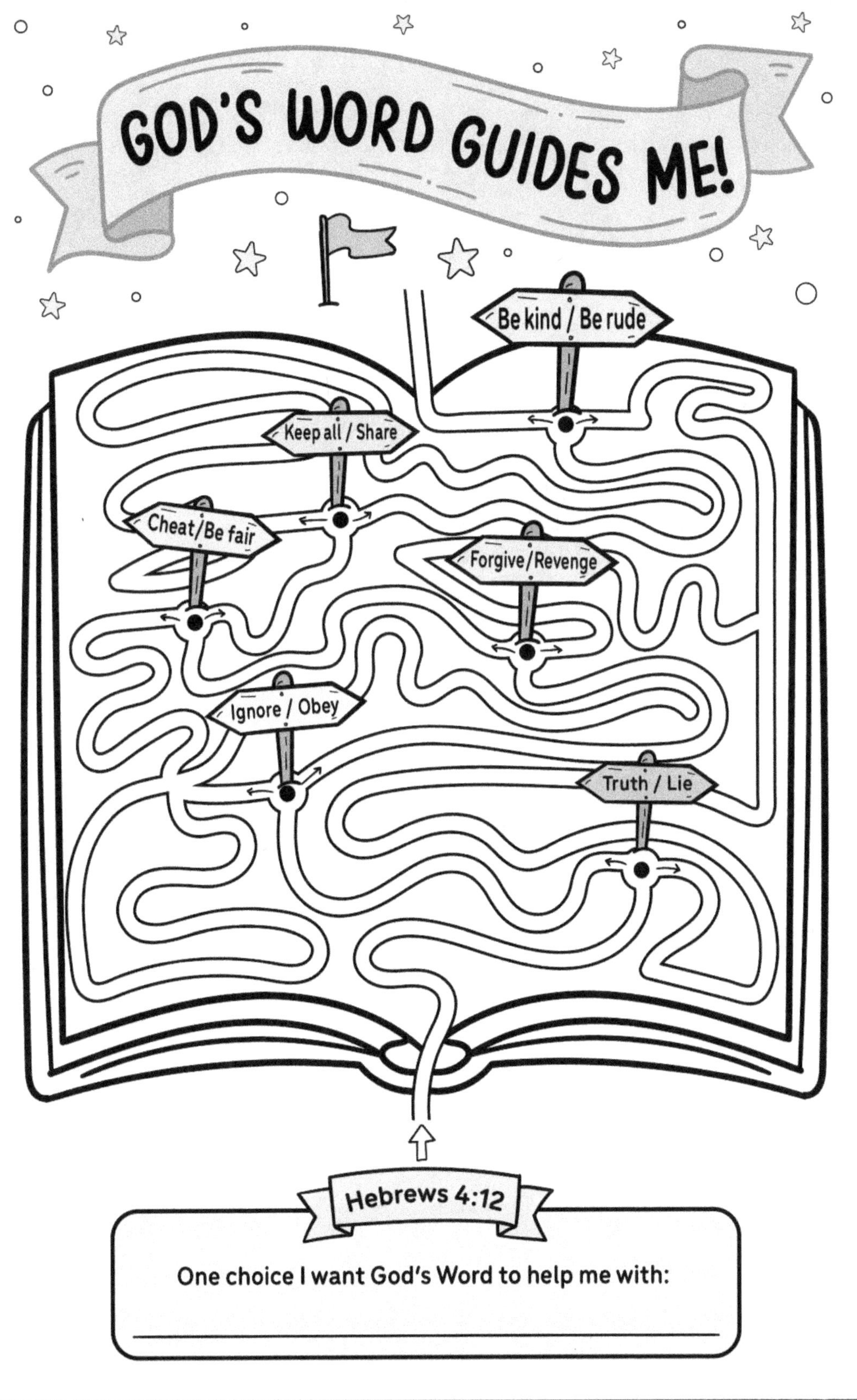

GOD'S WORD GUIDES ME!
Be kind / Be rude
Keep all / Share
Cheat/Be fair
Forgive/Revenge
Ignore / Obey
Truth / Lie
Hebrews 4:12
One choice I want God's Word to help me with:

WEEK 9
Remember God's Words

"I have hidden your word in my heart that I might not sin against you." - Psalm 119:11

BIG TRUTH: When you remember God's Word, it helps you choose what is right.

WARM-UP: Have you ever forgotten something important? Maybe your homework, your lunch, or what you were supposed to do first. Forgetting can make life harder.

Now think about something else: sometimes the problem isn't that we forgot our shoes. Sometimes we forget what God says is true.

Psalm 119:11 shows a smart plan: **store God's Word in your heart.**

What Psalm 119:11 Is Saying

The verse says: "I have hidden your word in my heart ..."

"Hidden" is like saving something valuable. Think about:

- ✝ putting money in a safe place
- ✝ saving your favorite pictures
- ✝ keeping a special letter
- ✝ protecting something you don't want to lose

God's Word is worth keeping. So the writer isn't only reading it once. He's keeping it close.

Then the verse says why: "that I might not sin against you."

This does not mean memorizing a verse makes you perfect. It means God's Word helps you fight sin. It gives you truth when lies feel tempting. It gives you a better choice when you feel pulled toward the wrong one.

What Does "In My Heart" Mean?

In the Bible, "heart" means more than feelings. It means the inside of you:

- ✝ your thoughts
- ✝ your choices
- ✝ what you love
- ✝ what you want
- ✝ what you believe

So storing God's Word in your heart means you let Scripture shape your inside, not just your outside.

Why Memorizing Helps

When you memorize God's Word, you can use it anytime:

- ✝ when you feel angry
- ✝ when you feel afraid
- ✝ when friends pressure you
- ✝ when you're tempted to lie
- ✝ when you feel alone

You don't have to open a Bible in the middle of a stressful moment to remember what God says. The verse is already with you.

A Kid Picture That Helps

Think about a flashlight. A flashlight is most helpful when it's already charged and ready. If it's dead, it won't help you in the dark.

God's Word stored in your heart is like having light ready when life feels dark or confusing.

How to Store God's Word

You don't need to memorize huge chunks at first. Start small:

1. Pick one verse.

2. Read it out loud three times.

3. Cover part of it and try again.

4. Say it once in the morning and once at night.

5. Ask a grown-up to quiz you kindly.

Little by little, you build a strong habit.

Tiny Step to Try This Week

Choose one short verse (it can be Psalm 119:11 or another from your Bible). Practice it for seven days. Write it on a card if that helps.

WORKBOOK ACTIVITIES

1) Verse Copy (Handwriting Practice)

Copy the Bible focus verse:

"I have hidden your word in my heart that I might not sin against you."

Psalm 119:11

Copy it one more time:

____

____

____

2) Fill in the Missing Words

"I have ______________________________ your _______________

in my ________________that I might not __________against you."

Word bank: hidden, word, heart, sin

3) **True or False**

Circle **True** or **False**.

1. God's Word is worth keeping.   **True / False**

2. Storing God's Word in my heart can help me avoid

    sin.   **True / False**

3. Memorizing Scripture means I will never mess up

    again.   **True / False**

4. God's Word can help me in everyday moments.   **True / False**

4) **What Would Help Most? (Circle One)**

If you feel...

1. Angry, God's Word can help you:

    A) explode

    B) choose self-control

    C) get revenge

2. Scared, God's Word can help you:

    A) hide forever

    B) trust God

    C) pretend God isn't there

3. Tempted to lie, God's Word can help you:

    A) blame others

    B) tell the truth

    C) make excuses

5) **My Memory Plan (Choose One)**

Pick one plan you will try this week and circle it:

    A) Say the verse 3 times each morning

    B) Say the verse 3 times each night

    C) Write the verse once each day

    D) Ask someone to quiz me every other day

Write your choice here:

____

____

____

6) "Store It Up" Challenge

Write Psalm 119:11 with some words missing. Then try to fill them in without looking.

"I have hidden your ______________________________

in my ______________________________________ ,

that I might not ______________________________ against you."

Now check and correct anything you missed.

7) Heart Storage (Reflection)

Write 3 reasons you want God's Word in your heart:

1. ____

2. ____

3. ____

8) Prayer Practice

Write a prayer (4–7 lines):

"God, thank You for Your Word.

____

____

____

Help me store it in my heart.

____

____

____

____

When I am tempted to sin, help me remember what You said.

____

____

____

Help me choose what is right. Amen."

9) **Knowledge Check (One-Minute Review)**

Answer in one short sentence:

What does Psalm 119:11 teach you to do?

____

____

____

____

____

Store God's Word in Your Heart!

Psalm 119:11

in my heart

hidden

your word

not sin

I have

against you.

that I

might

check yourself: *"I have hidden your word in my heart that I might not sin against you."*

WEEK 10
Follow God's Way

"Do not merely listen to the word, and so deceive yourselves. Do what it says." - James 1:22

BIG TRUTH: God wants you to obey His Word, not just hear it.

WARM-UP: Have you ever learned how to do something, like riding a bike, shooting a basketball, or baking cookies, by only listening to instructions?

Probably not. You can listen to directions all day, but you won't really learn until you try. You learn by doing.

James 1:22 says God's Word works like that too. It's not enough to hear it. God calls us to obey it.

What James 1:22 Is Saying

The verse says: "Be doers of the word, and not hearers only..."

A "hearer" is someone who listens but stops there. A "doer" is someone who listens and then takes action.

Then the verse gives a warning: "deceiving yourselves."

That means you can fool yourself into thinking you're doing great just because you know Bible facts. You might say the right answers but still ignore what God says.

God cares about what you know, but He also cares about what you do with what you know.

Why God Calls Us to Obey

Obedience is not how we earn God's love. God's love is a gift.

But obedience is one way we show that we trust God. When you obey, you're saying: "God, You are wise. Your way is good. I want to follow You."

Obedience is also protection. God's commands are not meant to ruin your fun. God's commands help you avoid sin and harm.

Hearing Can Be Easier Than Doing

It's often easy to hear a lesson and say, "That was nice."

It's harder to do things like:

✝ tell the truth when you could hide it

✝ forgive someone who hurt you

✝ stop gossip

✝ obey your parents with a good attitude

✝ be kind to someone who is annoying

That's why we need God's help. The Holy Spirit helps God's children grow. You don't obey alone.

A Kid Picture That Helps

Imagine a coach tells a team, "Keep your eyes on the ball." If the team nods and says, "Great idea," but never does it, they won't play well.

God's Word is not only information. It's guidance for real life.

What Does "Follow God's Way" Look Like?

It can look simple, like:

✝ using respectful words

✝ admitting when you were wrong

✝ sharing

✝ praying before you react

✝ choosing what is right even when friends don't

Small obedience steps matter. They add up.

Tiny Step to Try This Week

Pick one verse from the Bible this week. Ask: "What is one thing I can do because of this?" Then do it.

1) Verse Copy (Handwriting Practice)

Copy the Bible focus verse:

"Do not merely listen to the word, and so deceive yourselves. Do what it says." - **James 1:22**

Copy it one more time:

____

____

____

____

2) Fill in the Blanks

"Do not merely _______________________ to the word, and so

_______________________ yourselves"

Word bank: listen, deceive

3) Listen or Deceive? (Circle One)

1. A kid receives to a Bible lesson and then ignores it.

   Listen / Deceive

2. A kid reads a verse about kindness and then encourages someone.   **Listen / Deceive**

3. A kid knows verses about honesty but keeps lying.

   Listen / Deceive

4. A kid prays, asks God for help, and obeys even when it's hard.

   Listen / Deceive

4) One Step I Can Take

Write one Bible command you already know (in kid words).

Example: "Tell the truth." "Be kind." "Forgive."

My command: ____

____

____

Now write one action step you can do this week:

____

____

5) **Real-Life Choices (Circle the Best Next Step)**

1. You're tempted to join gossip.

    A) join in

    B) walk away or change the subject

2. You broke a rule and feel nervous.

    A) hide it

    B) tell the truth and ask forgiveness

3. You feel angry at your sibling.

    A) yell

    B) pause, pray, then speak calmly

4. Someone is left out.

    A) ignore them

    B) include them

6) **"Doing" Plan (Make It Specific)**

Fill in the blanks:

This week, I will obey God

by ____

on (day/time) _______________________________ with God's help.

7) Prayer Practice

Write a prayer (4–7 lines):

"God, thank You for Your Word.

____

____

Help me not only hear it, but obey it.

____

____

Show me one thing I should do this week.

____

____

Give me strength to follow Your way.

____

____

Amen."

8) Quick Review

Answer in one short sentence:

Why is it not enough to only hear God's Word?

____

____

____

9) Knowledge Check (One-Minute Review)

Answer in one short sentence:

What does James 1:22 teach you to do?

____

____

____

Be a Doer of the Word!

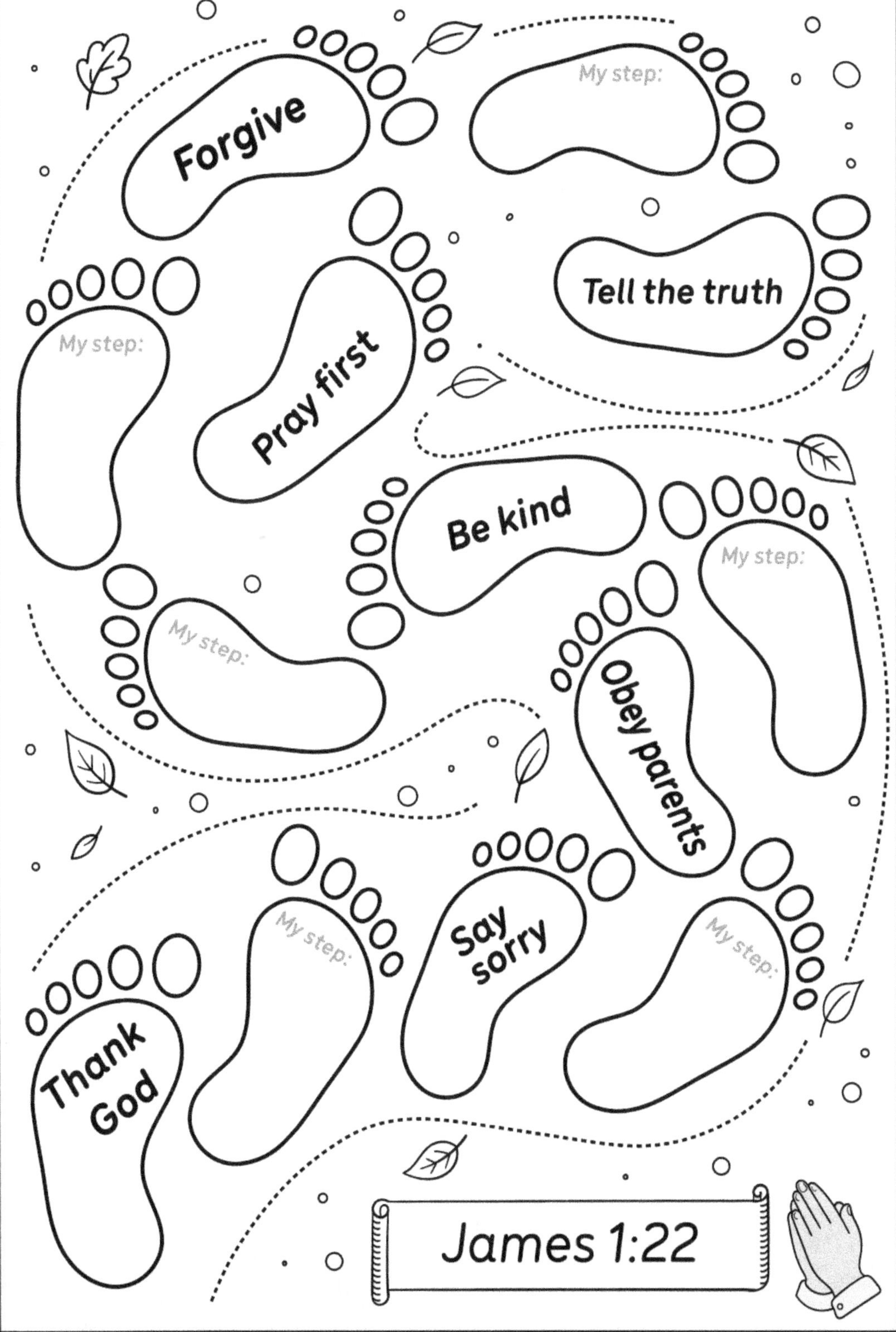

WEEK 11
Treasure God's Promises

"Have I not commanded you? Be strong and courageous. Do not be afraid; do not be discouraged, for the Lord your God will be with you wherever you go." - Joshua 1:9

BIG TRUTH: God's promises are precious, and God is with His people when they feel afraid.

WARM-UP: Have you ever had to do something that felt scary?

Maybe it was:

- ✟ starting a new school
- ✟ walking into a room where you don't know anyone
- ✟ taking a hard test
- ✟ sleeping alone at night
- ✟ standing up for someone

When you feel nervous, it helps to know someone is with you.

Joshua 1:9 is a promise-filled verse that speaks right into fearful moments.

What Joshua 1:9 Is Saying

God told Joshua, "Be strong and courageous." Joshua had a big job. He was leading God's people into a new land. That's a lot of responsibility.

God didn't tell Joshua to be brave because Joshua was naturally fearless. God told Joshua to be brave because God gave him a promise:

"For the Lord your God is with you wherever you go."

That's the key. Courage grows when you remember who is with you.

What Is a Promise?

A promise is a strong statement you can trust. People sometimes break promises, but God does not. When God promises something, it is safe.

God's promises are like:

- a strong rope when you feel like you might fall
- a steady light when you feel unsure
- a firm hand when you feel shaky

God's promises don't always mean life will be easy. But they do mean you are not alone and God will be faithful.

Courage Is Not the Same as "No Fear"

Some kids think brave people never feel fear. That's not true.

Courage means you do what is right even when you feel afraid.

You can feel nervous and still:

- tell the truth
- apologize
- try again
- include someone who is left out
- pray and trust God

Joshua probably felt nervous too. But God gave him a promise to hold onto.

"Wherever You Go" Matters

This promise is not only for one place. It says "wherever."

That means:

✟ at school

✟ at home

✟ on a trip

✟ at practice

✟ at the doctor

✟ when you're alone in your room

God is with His people in every place. You cannot walk outside His care.

How to Treasure God's Promises

To treasure something means you treat it as valuable.

You can treasure God's promises by:

✟ writing them down

✟ memorizing them

✟ praying them back to God

✟ reminding yourself of them when fear shows up

Here's a simple courage prayer from Joshua 1:9: "God, You are with me. Help me be strong and courageous."

Tiny Step to Try This Week

Pick one moment each day when you feel nervous. Whisper Joshua 1:9 (or part of it) and take one brave step.

WORKBOOK ACTIVITIES

1) Verse Copy (Handwriting Practice)

Copy the Bible focus verse:

"Have I not commanded you? Be strong and courageous. Do not be afraid; do not be discouraged, for the Lord your God will be with you wherever you go." - **Joshua 1:9**

Copy it one more time:

____

____

____

____

2) Fill in the Missing Words

"Be _______________________ and _______________________... for the LORD
your God is _________________________________ you wherever you go."

Word bank: strong, courageous, with

3) True or False

Circle **True** or **False**.

1. God sometimes leaves His people alone.   **True / False**

2. God's promises are worth treasuring.   **True / False**

3. Courage means I never feel fear.   **True / False**

4. God can help me take brave steps.   **True / False**

4) Courage Moments

Write three situations that can feel scary to you:

1. ____

2. ____

3. ____

Now write "God is with me" next to each one.

5) What Should I Do? (Circle the Best Choice)

1. You are nervous about a test.

    A) panic and quit

    B) pray, study, and do your best

2. You see someone being picked on.

    A) laugh so you fit in

    B) get help or stand with the person

3. You made a mistake and feel embarrassed.

    A) lie about it

    B) tell the truth and learn from it

4. You feel lonely.

    A) keep it inside forever

    B) talk to God and reach out to someone safe

6) Promise Treasure Chest

Write **four** promises from Joshua 1:9 (in your own words):

1. God says: _______________________________________

____

2. God says: _______________________________________

____

3. God says: _______________________________________

____

4. God says: _______________________________________

____

Now star the one you want to remember most: ★

7) My Courage Shield Words

Write 6–10 short words you want on a "courage shield."

Examples: "God is with me." "Be strong." "I can trust God."

My shield words:

____

____

____

____

8) **Prayer Practice**

Write a prayer (4–7 lines):

"God, thank You for Your promises.

____

____

____

When I feel afraid about

____

____

____

help me remember You are with me.

____

____

____

Help me be strong and courageous.

____

____

____

Amen."

9) **Knowledge Check (One-Minute Review)**

Answer in one short sentence:

What does Joshua 1:9 teach you to remember when you feel afraid?

____

____

____

____

Be Strong and Courageous
Joshua 1:9

God is with me when I feel _______________________________________.

God is with me at ____.

God is with me when I have to __________________________________.

God is with me when I'm worried about ___________________________.

God is with me when I need to say _______________________________.

God is with me wherever I _______________________________________.

PART THREE
People, Sin, and God's Plan

WEEK 12
Celebrate Being God's Image-Bearer

"So God created mankind in his own image, in the image of God he created them; male and female he created them." - Genesis 1:27

BIG TRUTH: You were made in God's image, so your life has value, purpose, and dignity.

WARM-UP: Have you ever compared yourself to someone else? Maybe you thought:

✝ "They're smarter than me."

✝ "They're better at sports than me."

✝ "They're more popular."

✝ "They're prettier."

✝ "They're funnier."

Comparing can make you feel proud for a minute or sad for a long time.

Genesis 1:27 gives you a better place to stand. It says something true about every person; something that doesn't change based on grades, skills, looks, or popularity.

What Genesis 1:27 Is Saying

This verse tells us that God created people in His own image.

That does **not** mean God looks like us the way a human looks. God is spirit. God is not limited to a body like ours.

So what does "image of God" mean?

It means God made people to **reflect** Him in special ways.

Here are a few ways humans reflect God:

- ✟ **We can think and learn.** We can ask questions and understand truth.
- ✟ **We can love.** We can care, show kindness, and build friendships.
- ✟ **We can choose.** We can make real decisions, not just act by instinct.
- ✟ **We can create.** We can build, draw, write, invent, and design.
- ✟ **We can know God.** Animals are part of creation and matter to God, but people are invited to know Him and worship Him.

That's a big deal. It means your life is not an accident. It means you are not "worthless." It means no one is "better human" than someone else.

"Male and Female He Created Them"

Genesis 1:27 also says God created people as male and female. God made both with value and purpose. Boys and girls both matter. Boys and girls both can know God, love God, and serve God.

The Image of God Changes How You Treat People

If every person is made in God's image, it changes how you treat them.

It means:

- ✟ bullying is never "just a joke"
- ✟ name-calling is not small
- ✟ using someone for your own fun is wrong
- ✟ ignoring someone who is hurting is not loving

It also changes how you treat *yourself.*

You should not hate yourself. You should not talk about yourself like you are trash. You can be honest about your sins and weaknesses, but you can also remember:**God made you, and your life matters.**

Image-Bearers Are Not Perfect

Being made in God's image does not mean you are perfect. People sin. People hurt each other. People make bad choices.

But even when people sin, they still have value as image-bearers. This is one reason God's rescue plan matters so much—He is saving real people with real worth.

Tiny Step to Try This Week

Each morning this week, say one true sentence: "God made me in His image. Help me reflect You today."

WORKBOOK ACTIVITIES

1) Verse Copy (Handwriting Practice)

Copy the Bible focus verse:

"So God created mankind in his own image, in the image of God he created them; male and female he created them." - **Genesis 1:27**

Copy it one more time:

____

____

____

____

2) Fill in the Blanks

"So God created mankind in his own ____________________________ "

Genesis 1:27

Write the missing word: _______________________________________

3) True or False

Circle **True** or **False**.

1. My value comes from how popular I am. **True / False**

2. Every person has value because God made them. **True / False**

3. Being made in God's image means I should treat
    others with respect.   **True / False**

4. Only adults are made in God's image.   **True / False**

4) Reflect God (Match It)

Match each "reflect" action to an example in the list below. Write down the letters.

Reflecting God:

1. Love
2. Truth
3. Creativity
4. Kindness
5. Wisdom

Examples:

A) making a card for someone

B) telling the truth even when it's hard

C) helping a new kid feel welcome

D) choosing a wise response instead of yelling

E) caring when someone is sad

5) Image-Bearer Respect (Circle the Best Choice)

1. Someone is different from you.

    A) make fun of them
    B) treat them with respect

2. You feel upset with yourself.

    A) say cruel things about yourself
    B) talk to God and remember you have value

3. You see someone sitting alone.

    A) ignore them
    B) invite them to join you

4. Someone makes a mistake.

> A) embarrass them

> B) show patience and help

6) "God Made Me" List

Write **five** good gifts God gave you (these can be abilities, traits, or opportunities).

1. ____

    ____

2. ____

    ____

3. ____

    ____

4. ____

    ____

5. ____

    ____

Now circle one gift you want to use for God this week.

7) My Reflection Plan

Finish the sentences:

> ✠ Today I can reflect God by showing love when_______________ .

> ✠ Today I can reflect God by telling the truth about _________ .

> ✠ Today I can reflect God by being kind to _______________ .

8) Prayer Practice

Write a prayer (4–7 lines):

"God, thank You for making me in Your image.

____

____

Help me see my value the right way.

____

____

Help me treat others with respect.

____

____

Help me reflect You in what I say and do.

____

____

Amen."

9) Knowledge Check (One-Minute Review)

Answer in one short sentence:

What does it mean that you are made in God's image?

____

____

____

____

____

____

____

Made in God's Image

My name: ______________________________

One way I can reflect God today: ______________________________

One kind thing I can do: ______________________________

Word Search

LOVE,   CARE,

KIND,   HONOR,

TRUTH,   HELP,

WISE,   JOY,

CREATE,   PEACE,

SERVE,   PRAY

L	C	B	M	R	Q	L	N	P	S	E	Z
D	R	N	H	O	N	O	R	K	E	P	B
L	E	W	W	T	V	S	P	I	R	R	C
O	A	I	Q	R	D	D	E	N	V	A	A
V	T	S	D	U	K	J	A	D	E	Y	R
E	E	E	G	T	N	Q	C	Q	U	R	E
O	J	O	Y	H	J	H	E	L	P	O	D
M	R	A	X	L	O	B	X	P	J	P	L

Genesis 1:27 — God made you to reflect Him.

WEEK 13
Tell the Truth About Sin

"For all have sinned and fall short of the glory of God." -
Romans 3:23

BIG TRUTH: Sin is real, sin is serious, and every person has sinned, so we all need God's help and forgiveness.

WARM-UP: Have you ever tried really hard to do the right thing... and still messed up?

Maybe you:

✝ said you wouldn't get angry, but you did

✝ promised you'd tell the truth, but you lied

✝ tried to be kind, but you were rude

✝ wanted to obey, but you complained

That feeling can make you want to hide. Or it can make you want to blame someone else.

Romans 3:23 tells the truth in a clear way. And even though it's a serious truth, it's also a helpful one, because the truth leads us to God.

What Romans 3:23 Is Saying

The verse says, "For **all** have sinned..."

"All" means everyone. Not just "bad people." Not just adults. Not just kids who get in trouble a lot. Everyone.

Then it says, "and fall short of the glory of God."

"Fall short" is like missing the goal. It's like aiming for the center of a target and not hitting it.

God's "glory" is His perfect goodness and holiness. God is always right. God is always pure. God is always loving. When we sin, we fall short of God's perfect standard.

What Sin Is (In Kid Words)

Sin is when we go against God's ways.

Sin can be:

- ✝ **doing something God says not to do** (like lying)
- ✝ **not doing what God says to do** (like refusing to love your neighbor)
- ✝ **wanting the wrong thing in your heart** (like jealousy or pride)

Sin is not only "big crimes." Sin can also be ordinary wrong choices that start inside us.

Why We Need to Tell the Truth About Sin

Sometimes people try to make sin sound small.

They say things like:

- ✝ "It's no big deal."
- ✝ "Everyone does it."
- ✝ "It's fine as long as you don't get caught."

But sin is serious because it harms:

- ✝ our relationship with God
- ✝ our relationships with people
- ✝ our own hearts

Sin is like a crack in a glass. One crack might seem small, but it makes the whole glass weaker.

The Good News Hides Nearby

Romans 3:23 is not the end of the story.

The Bible tells the truth about sin so we won't pretend. But the Bible also tells us about God's mercy and Jesus' rescue.

When you admit sin, you are not announcing that you are hopeless. You are saying, "I need help." And God loves to help His children.

What You Can Do When You Sin

Here are three wise steps:

1. **Admit it.** Don't hide or make excuses.

2. **Confess it to God.** Tell Him the truth.

3. **Turn back.** Ask God to help you do what is right next.

God does not want you stuck in shame. God wants you to come into the light.

Tiny Step to Try This Week

Each day, ask yourself one gentle question: "God, what do You want me to confess today?"

Then pray honestly and take one step to make it right.

WORKBOOK ACTIVITIES

1) Verse Copy (Handwriting Practice)

Copy the Bible focus verse:

"For all have sinned and fall short of the glory of God." –
Romans 3:23

Copy it one more time:

____

____

____

2) Fill in the Blanks

"For all have _____________ and fall ________ of the glory of God."

Word bank: sinned, short

3) True or False

Circle **True** or **False**.

1. Only adults sin. **True / False**
2. Sin can be in actions and in attitudes. **True / False**
3. Telling the truth about sin helps us come to God. **True / False**
4. If I sin, I should hide from God forever. **True / False**

4) "Fall Short" Target Check

Read each example. Circle **Sin** or **Not sin**.

1. Telling the truth even when it's hard **Sin / Not sin**
2. Cheering when someone fails **Sin / Not sin**
3. Sharing with a friend **Sin / Not sin**
4. Lying to stay out of trouble **Sin / Not sin**
5. Praying for someone **Sin / Not sin**
6. Being rude to your parents **Sin / Not sin**

5) Sin Can Look Like... (Sort It)

Write each word in either the sin or no sin row:

Words: lying, kindness, jealousy, obedience, gossip, gratitude, stealing, forgiveness, pride, patience

Sin: ____

____

____

Not sin: ____

____

____

6) What Should I Do Next? (Circle One)

1. You lied and now you feel nervous.

    A) pretend nothing happened
    B) tell the truth and ask forgiveness

2. You were mean online.

    A) delete it and move on

    B) confess, apologize, and make it right

3. You feel jealous of a friend.

    A) act nice but feel angry inside

    B) tell God and ask for a thankful heart

7) **Confession Practice**

Write one thing you want to confess to God (you can keep it general):

I want to confess: ____

____

Now write a short prayer (3–6 lines):

"God, I confess ____

____

Please forgive me.

____

____

Help me turn away from sin and choose what is right.

____

____

Amen."

8) **Knowledge Check (One-Minute Review)**

Answer in one short sentence:

What does Romans 3:23 teach you about people and sin?

____

____

____

____

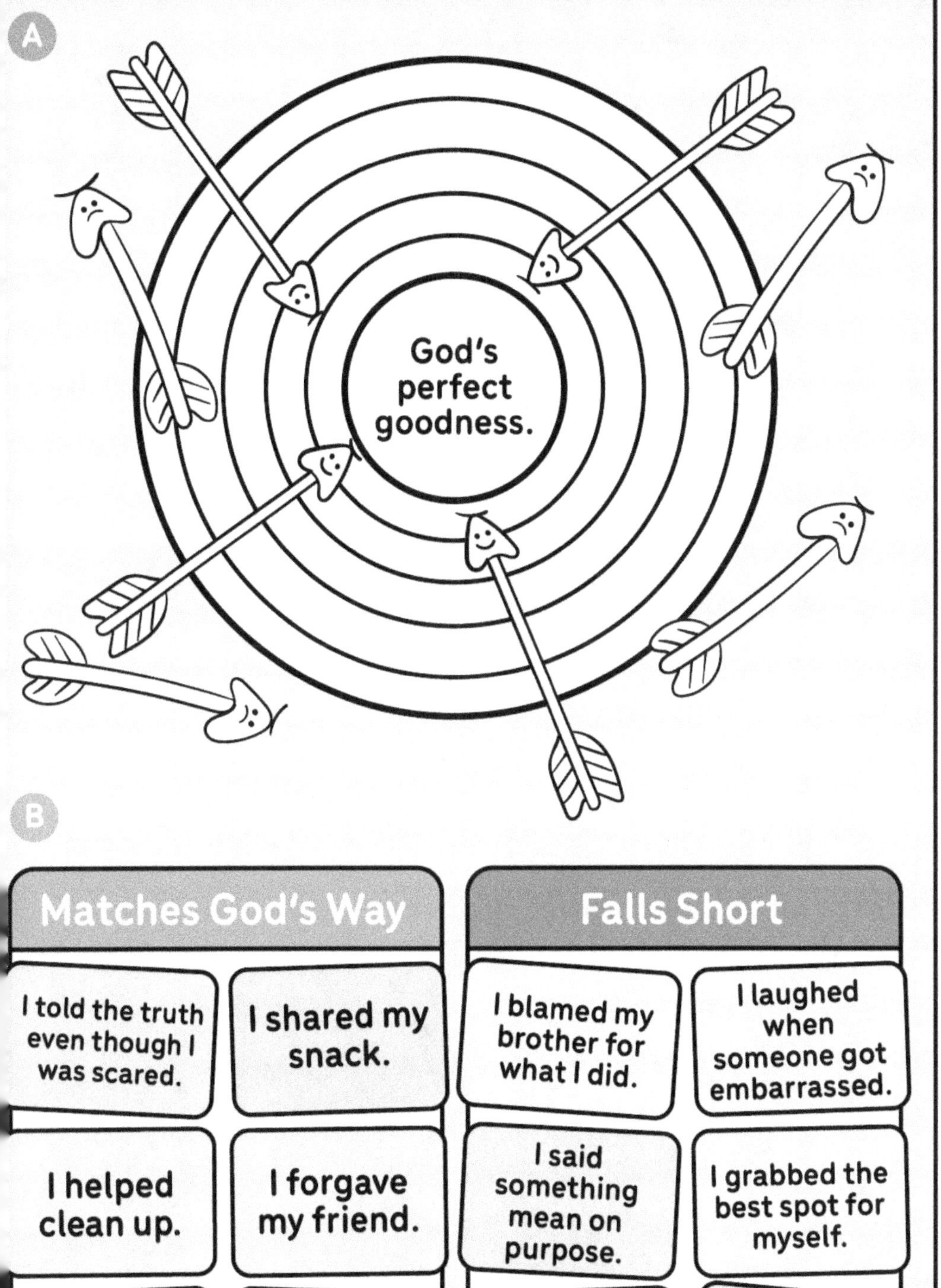

A
God's perfect goodness.
B
Matches God's Way
Falls Short
I told the truth even though I was scared.
I shared my snack.
I blamed my brother for what I did.
I laughed when someone got embarrassed.
I helped clean up.
I forgave my friend.
I said something mean on purpose.
I grabbed the best spot for myself.
I obeyed right away.
I used kind words.
I hid my mistake.
I lied to stay out of trouble.
Romans 3:23 — We all need God's help.

WEEK 14
See What Sin Breaks

"But your iniquities have separated you from your God; your sins have hidden his face from you, so that he will not hear." - Isaiah 59:2

BIG TRUTH: Sin separates us from God and harms relationships, but God invites us to come back through confession and repentance.

WARM-UP: Have you ever had a fight with someone you care about? Maybe a friend, a sibling, or a parent. Even if you're in the same house, something can feel "far" between you. The relationship feels strained.

Isaiah 59:2 explains something like that on a bigger level. Sin doesn't only break rules. Sin breaks relationship.

What Isaiah 59:2 Is Saying

The verse says, "But your iniquities have separated you from your God..."

"Iniquities" is another word for sins, wrong choices and wrong desires.

This verse teaches that sin creates a **separation** between people and God. God is holy, which means He is perfectly pure and always right. Sin does not belong with God's holiness.

So sin does something serious:it pushes us away from God.

What Separation Feels Like

Separation from God doesn't always feel like thunder and lightning. Sometimes it feels quiet.

It can look like:

- ✝ not wanting to pray
- ✝ feeling guilty and trying to hide
- ✝ making excuses instead of confessing
- ✝ getting used to sin so it doesn't feel "wrong" anymore
- ✝ feeling empty even when you're busy

Sin can also break relationships with people.

When sin shows up, it can cause:

- ✝ lies → broken trust
- ✝ anger → hurtful words
- ✝ jealousy → bitterness
- ✝ selfishness → fighting
- ✝ gossip → ruined friendships

Sin breaks things on the inside and the outside.

A Kid Picture That Helps

Picture a bridge that connects two sides of a river. If the bridge breaks, people can't cross easily. They might shout from far away, but they can't walk close.

Sin is like that. It creates a gap between us and God.

But here is the important truth: God does not leave us with a broken bridge and say, "Too bad." God shows us the way back.

Confession and Repentance (Simple Definitions)

These are important Bible words, and you can learn them.

- ✝ **Confession** means telling the truth to God about your sin. No hiding. No excuses.
- ✝ **Repentance** means turning around. You turn away from sin and turn back to God.

Confession says, "God, I did wrong." Repentance says, "God, help me change direction."

God Wants You to Come Back

Isaiah 59:2 is serious, but it is not meant to make you hopeless. It is meant to show you what sin does so you won't pretend.

God wants His children close. When you confess and repent, you are coming into the light.

And the Bible's big story points to Jesus, the One who brings us back to God. We'll talk more about that as we keep going, but here's the point for this week:

Don't hide. Come back.

Tiny Step to Try This Week

If you notice sin this week, pause and do this:

1. Admit it.

2. Confess it to God.

3. Turn and take one right step.

WORKBOOK ACTIVITIES

1) Verse Copy (Handwriting Practice)

Copy the Bible focus verse:

"But your iniquities have separated you from your God; your sins have hidden his face from you, so that he will not hear." - **Isaiah 59:2**

Copy it one more time:

____

____

____

____

2) Fill in the Blank

"Your iniquities have ______________ you from your God."

Write the missing word: ____________________________________

3) True or False

Circle **True** or **False**.

1. Sin can separate people from God.   True / False

2. Confession means hiding your sin.   True / False

3. Repentance means turning away from sin.   True / False

4. Sin can hurt relationships with people too.   True / False

4) Match the Word to the Meaning

Draw lines to match.

1. Sin   A) turning back to God and away from sin

2. Separation   B) wrong choices and wrong desires

3. Confession   C) a gap in relationship

4. Repentance   D) telling the truth to God

5) What Does Sin Break? (Write Two Examples)

Write two ways sin can break trust or friendship:

1. ____

   ____

2. ____

   ____

Now write one way you can help fix what sin breaks:

____

____

____

6) **Scenario Sorting (Circle the Best Next Step)**

1. You lied to stay out of trouble.

    A) keep lying

    B) confess and tell the truth

2. You hurt someone's feelings.

    A) say "whatever"

    B) apologize and ask forgiveness

3. You feel guilty and don't want to pray.

    A) avoid God

    B) pray anyway and confess

4. You're jealous of a friend.

    A) treat them coldly

    B) tell God and ask for a thankful heart

7) **Build a Bridge Back (Reflection)**

Fill in the blanks:

When I sin, I can come back to God by:

1. ______________________________________ (telling the truth to God)

2. ______________________________________ (turning around)

Now write one short sentence:

"This week, I will come back to God when

____

____

8) **Prayer Practice**

Write a prayer (5–8 lines):

"Holy God, I'm sorry for my sin.

____

____

Please forgive me for

____

____

Help me turn away from what is wrong.

____

____

Bring me close to You again.

____

____

Help me make things right with others too.

____

Amen."

9) Knowledge Check (One-Minute Review)

Answer in one short sentence:

What does Isaiah 59:2 teach you about sin?

____

____

____

____

____

____

Instructions: • Color the page. • Write on the planks.
• Draw the planks into the bridge to show the way back.
Me
God
Prayer
My step:
Confession
My step:
Prayer
My step:
Truth
Make it right
Forgiveness
Repentance
Isaiah 59:2

WEEK 15
Choose Wisdom Over Foolishness

"The fear of the Lord is the beginning of knowledge, but fools despise wisdom and instruction." - Proverbs 1:7

BIG TRUTH: Wisdom begins with respecting God, and foolish choices happen when we ignore God's instruction.

WARM-UP: Have you ever done something and then thought, "Why did I do that?"

Maybe you:

✝ said something mean without thinking

✝ joined in with friends even though it felt wrong

✝ ignored a warning and got in trouble

✝ rushed and made a mess

That's a good moment to learn. Proverbs is a Bible book full of wisdom for everyday life: school life, friend life, family life, and heart life.

Proverbs 1:7 tells you where wisdom starts.

What Proverbs 1:7 Is Saying

The verse says, "The fear of the LORD is the beginning of knowledge..."

In the Bible, "fear of the LORD" usually means deep respect. It means you take God seriously. You trust that God is wise, good, and in charge.

So, wisdom doesn't begin with "I know everything." Wisdom begins with:

"God knows everything, and I want to listen to Him."

Then the verse says, "fools despise wisdom and instruction."

A "fool" in Proverbs is not someone who struggles with school. It's not about grades.

A fool is someone who hears what is right and says:

- ✝ "I don't care."
- ✝ "I'll do what I want."
- ✝ "Nobody can tell me."

A fool doesn't just make a mistake once. A fool refuses to learn.

Wisdom vs. Foolishness (Kid Version)

Wisdom looks like:

- ✝ stopping to think before you act
- ✝ listening to godly instruction
- ✝ choosing what is right, even when friends don't
- ✝ learning from correction
- ✝ telling the truth
- ✝ asking God for help

Foolishness looks like:

- ✝ rushing without thinking
- ✝ ignoring warnings
- ✝ laughing at what is right
- ✝ refusing to say sorry
- ✝ doing wrong and calling it "fun"

Wisdom isn't about being perfect. Wisdom is about being teachable.

A Kid Picture That Helps

Imagine two kids standing near a sign that says: "Wet Paint."

- ✚ One kid respects the sign and walks around.
- ✚ The other kid touches the paint anyway and leaves a handprint. Then they blame the sign.

The sign wasn't the problem. The choice was.

God's instruction is like a loving warning sign. It helps you avoid trouble.

How Wisdom Grows

Wisdom grows when you practice three habits:

1. **Listen** - to God's Word and wise adults.
2. Think - "What could happen if I do this?"
3. Choose - the right step, even if it's harder.

Wisdom often looks boring at first, but later it feels peaceful.

Tiny Step to Try This Week

Before you decide something important this week, pause and ask: "Does this choice respect God?" Then choose the wise step.

WORKBOOK ACTIVITIES

1) Verse Copy (Handwriting Practice)

Copy the Bible focus verse:

"The fear of the Lord is the beginning of knowledge, but fools despise wisdom and instruction." - **Proverbs 1:7**

Copy it one more time:

____

____

____

____

2) Fill in the Blanks

"The fear of the LORD is the beginning of ________________ , but fools despise ________________________ and instruction."

Word bank:knowledge, wisdom

3) Match the Word to the Meaning

Draw lines to match.

1. Wisdom   A) refusing to learn and ignoring instruction

2. Foolishness   B) choosing what is right with God's help

3. Fear of the LORD   C) deep respect for God

4) Wise or Foolish? (Circle One)

1. You're tempted to cheat. You stop and choose honesty.   **Wise / Foolish**
2. Someone corrects you, and you refuse to listen.   **Wise / Foolish**
3. You pause and pray before you speak when you're angry.   **Wise / Foolish**
4. You join in teasing someone to look cool.   **Wise / Foolish**
5. You admit you were wrong and apologize.   **Wise / Foolish**

5) Two Choices, Two Results

Finish each sentence with your own words.

1. If I choose wisdom, it can lead to

____

____

2. If I choose foolishness, it can lead to

____

____

6) **What Would Wisdom Do? (Write One Wise Step)**

Write one wise step for each situation:

1. Friends pressure you to be unkind.

    Wise step:

    ____

    ____

2. You're frustrated with homework.

    Wise step:

    ____

    ____

3. You feel jealous of someone.

    Wise step:

    ____

    ____

4. You're about to argue with a sibling.

    Wise step:

    ____

    ____

7) **My Wisdom Plan**

Circle one instruction you want to take seriously this week:

    A) Use calm words

    B) Tell the truth

    C) Obey quickly

    D) Forgive

    E) Stop gossip

    F) Pray daily

Write it here: _______________________________________

Now write one way you will practice it:

____

____

8) Prayer Practice

Write a prayer (4–7 lines):

"God, You are wise and good.

____

____

Help me respect You.

____

____

Help me love wisdom and instruction.

____

____

When I'm tempted to act foolishly, help me choose what is right.

____

____

Amen."

9) Knowledge Check (One-Minute Review)

Answer in one short sentence:

What does Proverbs 1:7 teach you about wisdom?

____

____

____

____

____

Choose Wisdom!

Proverbs 1:7

Wise Choice

Foolish Choice

Wisdom leads to:

Foolishness leads to:

WEEK 16
Thank God for His Rescue Plan

"And I will put enmity between you and the woman, and between your offspring and hers; he will crush your head, and you will strike his heel." - Genesis 3:15

(Note: This verse includes a hard picture. We'll explain it in a careful, kid-safe way.)

BIG TRUTH: God promised a Rescuer, and He keeps His promises.

WARM-UP: Have you ever broken something and wished you could go back and fix it right away?

Maybe it was:

+ a friendship you hurt with your words

+ a rule you broke

+ a moment you wish you could redo

The Bible starts with a world God made good. Then sin entered, and everything changed. But here's the hope: right after sin showed up, God spoke a promise about rescue.

Genesis 3:15 is like the first small spark of the gospel, good news, shining in a dark moment.

What Happened in Genesis 3

In Genesis 3, Adam and Eve disobeyed God. They listened to the serpent's lie and chose sin. Sin brought shame, fear, and separation.

You might expect the story to end with, "That's it. You failed."

But that's not what God did.

God came looking for them. God spoke truth. God judged sin. And God also gave a promise:a Rescuer would come.

What Genesis 3:15 Is Saying (In Kid Words)

This verse is sometimes called "the first promise of the Savior."

It talks about a battle between:

- ✣ the serpent (who represents evil and the enemy of God's people), and

- ✣ the woman's offspring (a future person from her family line)

Then it says that this future offspring will "bruise your head." That sounds odd, but here's the meaning:

- ✣ A bruise to the heel hurts.

- ✣ A bruise to the head is a defeat.

So God was promising that evil would hurt the Rescuer, but the Rescuer would win in the end.

This promise points forward to Jesus.

God's Plan Was Not an Emergency

Sometimes people think God made the world, then sin happened, and God panicked.

But God did not panic.

God was not surprised. God already had a rescue plan. And He began to show it right there in Genesis.

That should comfort you. God is wise. God sees the whole story. Even when people make a mess, God can bring rescue and hope.

How the Rescue Plan Works

Here are the simple steps:

1. **God is holy and good.**

2. **People sinned.** We disobeyed God.

3. **Sin deserves judgment.** God is fair.

4. **God promised a Savior.** God is merciful.

5. **Jesus came.** He lived without sin.

6. **Jesus died and rose again.** He defeated sin and death.

You'll learn more details about Jesus in later weeks, but this week gives you the big idea:

God makes promises, and God keeps them.

Why This Matters to You

If God kept a rescue promise that started in Genesis, you can trust Him with your life too.

When you sin, you can confess and come back.

When you feel afraid, you can remember God is working.

When you feel stuck, you can remember God is not finished.

God's rescue plan is not just an old story. It's God's love at work.

Tiny Step to Try This Week

Each day, thank God for rescue with one short sentence: "God, thank You for sending the Rescuer."

WORKBOOK ACTIVITIES

1) Verse Copy (Handwriting Practice)

Copy a short portion of the Bible focus verse (kid-sized):

"He will crush your head…"_ **Genesis 3:15**

Copy it one more time:

____

____

____

____

2) What Happened First? (Number the Events)

Put these in order from 1–5.

____ God made the world good.

____ God promised a Rescuer.

____ Adam and Eve sinned.

____ Sin brought shame and separation.

____ God kept His promise by sending Jesus.

3) True or False

Circle **True** or **False**.

1. God was surprised by sin.   **True / False**
2. God promised a Rescuer in Genesis.   **True / False**
3. Evil will win forever.   **True / False**
4. God keeps His promises.   **True / False**

4) Big Word Helper

Match the word to its meaning.

1. Rescue   A) a promise God makes

2. Promise   B) saving someone who is in trouble

3. Savior/Rescuer   C) the One God sent to save His people

5) "God Keeps Promises" Check

Write three Bible promises you can remember (or write "I want to learn one" if you're not sure yet).

1. ____

2. ____

3. ____

6) **Connect the Dots (From Promise to Jesus)**

Draw lines to match.

1. Genesis 3:15   A) God's first rescue promise

2. Jesus   B) the promised Rescuer

3. Sin   C) what made rescue needed

4. God   D) the One who planned rescue

7) **My Thank-You List**

Write four things you can thank God for about His rescue plan:

____

____

____

____

8) **Prayer Practice**

Write a prayer (5–8 lines):

"God, thank You for loving Your people.

____

____

Thank You for promising a Rescuer.

____

____

Thank You for sending Jesus.

____

____

Help me trust Your plan when life feels hard.

____

____

Help me turn from sin and follow You.

Amen."

9) Knowledge Check (One-Minute Review)

Answer in one short sentence:

What is God's rescue plan?

God Kept His Rescue Promise!
Genesis 3:15

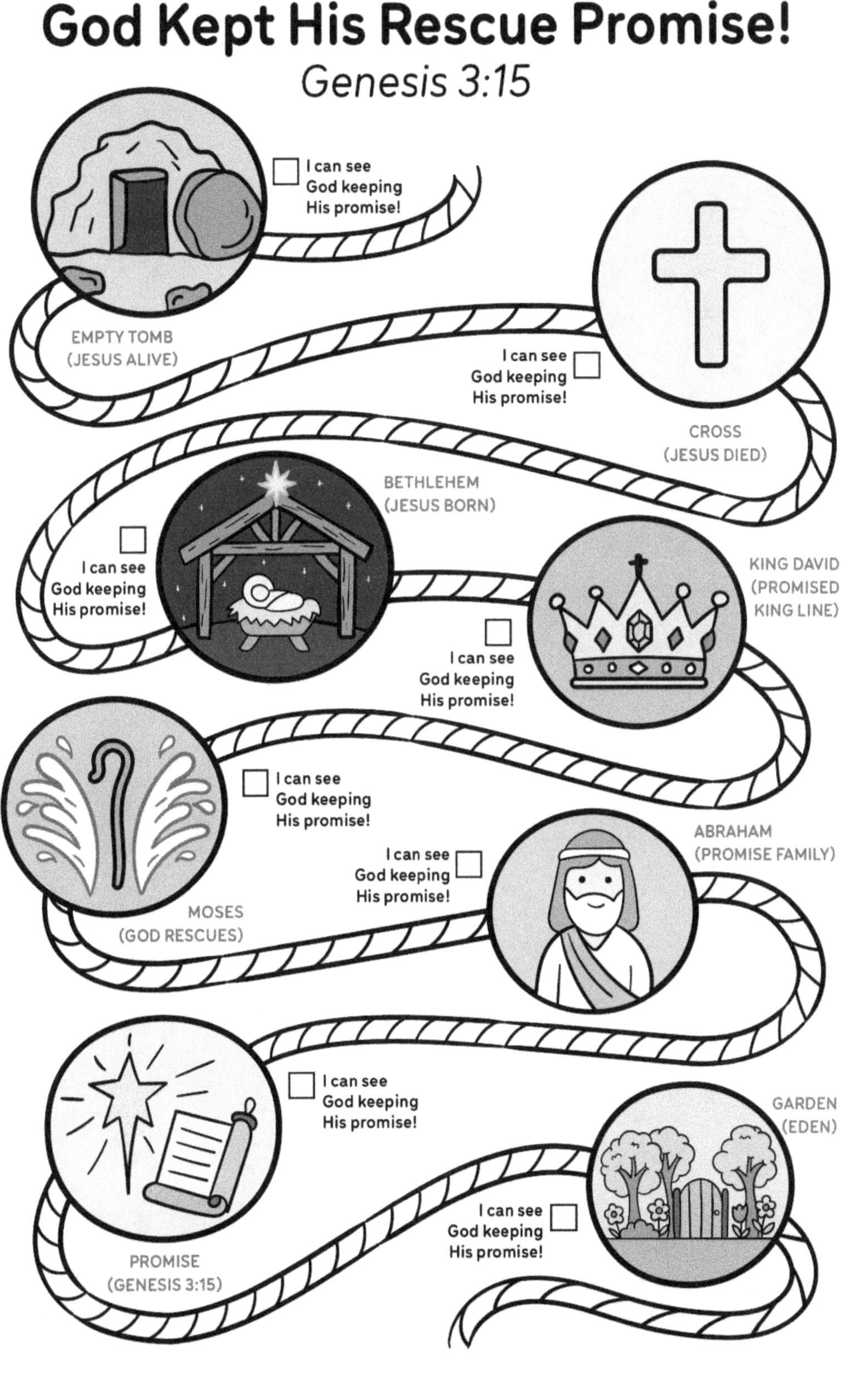

PART FOUR
Jesus Christ

WEEK 17
Welcome the Promised King

"Today in the town of David a Savior has been born to you; he is the Messiah, the Lord." - Luke 2:11

BIG TRUTH: Jesus is the promised Savior and King, and His birth is good news for everyone who will trust Him.

WARM-UP: Have you ever waited for something exciting, like a birthday, a trip, or a special surprise? Waiting can feel long. Sometimes you even count the days.

God's people waited a long time for a promised Savior. God had been promising rescue since Genesis. Prophets spoke about a coming King. People hoped and prayed and waited.

Then, in Luke 2, the waiting changed into joy.

What Luke 2:11 Is Saying

An angel appeared to shepherds at night and gave them a message:

"Today in the town of David a Savior has been born to you; he is the Messiah, the Lord."

That one sentence is packed with meaning.

- ✤ **"Today"** - This is real history, not a pretend story. A real baby was born.
- ✤ **"A Savior"** - Someone who rescues. Jesus came to save people from sin.
- ✤ **"The Messiah"** - The promised King God had spoken about.
- ✤ **"The Lord"** - Jesus is not only a helpful teacher. He is the Lord, worthy of worship and trust.

The angel wasn't sharing gossip. The angel was announcing **good news**.

Why Shepherds?

Shepherds were not famous or powerful. They worked outside. They were not the kind of people you'd expect to receive the first royal announcement.

But God chose them.

That shows something important about Jesus: He did not come only for rich people, important people, or perfect people. He came for ordinary people who need rescue.

That includes you and me.

What Kind of King Is Jesus?

When people hear "king," they might think of someone who:

✝ demands attention

✝ lives in comfort

✝ uses power to get what they want

But Jesus is a different kind of King.

Jesus is:

✝ **humble** – He was born in a simple place.

✝ **kind** – He cares for the weak and the hurting.

✝ **holy** – He always does what is right.

✝ **brave** – He came to face sin and death.

✝ **faithful** – He keeps God's promises.

Jesus is the promised King, but He didn't arrive with a gold crown and a fancy parade. He arrived as a baby, in humility, because His mission was rescue.

What Does It Mean to Welcome Jesus?

Welcoming Jesus doesn't mean setting out milk and cookies.

Welcoming Jesus means:

- ✝ believing He is who the Bible says He is
- ✝ trusting Him as Savior
- ✝ honoring Him as Lord
- ✝ listening to His words
- ✝ following Him in daily life

It also means joy. The angel's message was good news. Jesus brings hope, forgiveness, and peace with God.

Tiny Step to Try This Week

Each day, say one sentence to Jesus like this: "Jesus, You are the promised King. Help me welcome You today."

WORKBOOK ACTIVITIES

1) Verse Copy (Handwriting Practice)

Copy the Bible focus verse carefully:

"Today in the town of David a Savior has been born to you; he is the Messiah, the Lord." **Luke 2:11**

Copy it one more time:

____

____

____

____

2) Fill in the Blanks

"Today in the town of David a ______________ has been born to you,

He is the __________________ the Lord."

Word bank: Savior, Messiah

3) Word Helper (Match the Meaning)

Draw lines to match each word to its meaning.

1. Savior   A) the promised King

2. Christ   B) the One who rescues

3. Lord   C) the One in charge, worthy of worship

4. Good news   D) joyful message from God

4) True or False

Circle **True** or **False**.

1. Jesus was born to rescue people from sin.   **True / False**

2. Only important people can welcome Jesus.   **True / False**

3. Jesus is both Savior and King.   **True / False**

4. Jesus came with pride and showed off His power.   **True / False**

5) Who Heard the News First?

Circle the correct answer:

The angel first told the good news to:

    A) kings in a palace

    B) soldiers in a fort

    C) shepherds in the fields

Write one sentence about what that teaches you about God:

____

____

____

____

____

____

6) Welcome the King (Choose One Action)

Circle one way you can welcome Jesus this week:

    A) Pray each day

    B) Read one Gospel story

    C) Obey quickly at home

    D) Speak kindly when you're annoyed

    E) Tell someone one true thing about Jesus

Write what you chose: ____

Now write when you will do it: ___________________________________

____

____

7) Good News for Me

Finish the sentences:

✞ Jesus is good news because _____________________________________

____

✞ I need a Savior because ____

____

✞ Jesus is King, so I want to _____________________________________

____

8) Prayer Practice

Write a prayer (5–8 lines):

"Jesus, thank You for coming.

____

____

Thank You for being my Savior.

____

____

Thank You for being the promised King.

____

____

Help me welcome You with my words and choices this week.

____

____

Amen."

9) Knowledge Check (One-Minute Review)

Answer in one short sentence:

What does Luke 2:11 teach you about who Jesus is?

____

____

____

____

____

____

Welcome the Promised King!

Luke 2:11

WEEK 18
Believe Jesus Is God with Us

"The Word became flesh and made his dwelling among us. We have seen his glory, the glory of the one and only Son, who came from the Father, full of grace and truth." - John 1:14

BIG TRUTH: Jesus is God who came close. He became human and lived among people so we could know God's love and truth.

WARM-UP: Have you ever tried to explain something big to a younger kid? Sometimes you have to get down to their level. You use words they understand. You show them, not just tell them.

That idea can help you understand John 1:14.

God didn't only send messages from far away. God came close.

What John 1:14 Is Saying

This verse says, "The Word became flesh..."

In John's Gospel, "the Word" is a name for Jesus. It means Jesus is God's message, God's truth, and God's self-revealing Person.

So when it says "the Word became flesh," it means Jesus truly became human. Not pretend-human. Not a costume. Real flesh and blood—like us.

Jesus:

✝ got hungry and ate

✝ got tired and slept

✝ walked places with dusty feet

✝ felt pain

✝ cried

✝ laughed

✝ lived a real human life

And at the same time, Jesus is still God. That's why this is such amazing news.

What "Dwelt Among Us" Means

"Dwelt" means lived with, stayed with.

Jesus didn't come for a quick visit and then disappear. He lived among people. He talked with them. He ate with them. He listened. He helped. He healed.

This shows us God's heart. God is not far away and uninterested. God came near.

Why Jesus Coming Close Matters

Jesus is called "Immanuel," which means "God with us" (you'll see that in other places in the Bible).

God with us means:

✝ God understands human life

✝ God cares about real struggles

✝ God sees pain and sorrow

✝ God knows what temptation feels like

✝ God is not distant from His people

If you ever think, "God wouldn't understand how I feel," John 1:14 answers that.

Jesus came close on purpose.

Jesus Shows Us What God Is Like

Sometimes people say, "I believe in God," but they don't know what God is like.

Jesus shows us.

When you see Jesus:

    ✝ caring for the sick

    ✝ speaking truth

    ✝ welcoming children

    ✝ forgiving sinners

    ✝ standing against evil

    ✝ loving perfectly

You are seeing God's character in action.

How Do We Respond?

John 1:14 invites you to believe.

Believing is not just saying, "Sure, I guess that's true." Believing means trusting Jesus and welcoming Him.

You can say:

"Jesus, I believe You came close. Help me trust You today."

Tiny Step to Try This Week

Read one short story about Jesus in the Gospels (Matthew, Mark, Luke, or John). After you read it, write one sentence:

"This shows me God is

____

____

____

____

____

WORKBOOK ACTIVITIES

1) Verse Copy (Handwriting Practice)

Copy the Bible focus verse phrase:

"The Word became flesh and made his dwelling among us." **John 1:14**

Copy it one more time:

____

____

____

____

2) Fill in the Blanks

"The Word became ______________________________

and made his dwelling among ______________________."

Word bank: flesh, us

3) Match the Meaning

Draw lines to match.

1. The Word		A) lived with people
2. Became flesh		B) Jesus
3. Dwelt among us		C) became truly human

4) True or False

Circle **True** or **False**.

1. Jesus is God who came close. **True / False**
2. Jesus only pretended to be human. **True / False**
3. Jesus lived among people and understands real life. **True / False**
4. Jesus shows us what God is like. **True / False**

5) **Jesus Came Close (Circle All That Are True)**

Circle every true statement:

- ☩ Jesus got hungry.

- ☩ Jesus never felt tired.

- ☩ Jesus lived among people.

- ☩ Jesus understands what it's like to be tempted.

- ☩ Jesus came only for perfect people.

- ☩ Jesus showed God's love.

6) **"God With Us" Moments**

Write three moments when it helps to remember Jesus is God with us:

1. When I feel ____

    ____

2. When I am ____

    ____

3. When I need ____

    ____

Now finish this sentence:

"Jesus, You are with me when_______________________________________

_______________________________________ ."

7) **See God Through Jesus**

Pick one Jesus action and finish the sentence:

Jesus welcomed children, so God is _______________________________

____

Jesus forgave sinners, so God is _________________________________

____

Jesus told the truth, so God is _______________________

____

Jesus healed the hurting, so God is _______________________

____

(You can do more than one if you want.)

8) Prayer Practice

Write a prayer (5–8 lines):

"Jesus, thank You for coming close.

____

____

Thank You for becoming human and living among us.

____

____

Help me trust You when I feel

____

____

Help me remember You understand my life.

____

____

____

Amen."

9) Knowledge Check (One-Minute Review)

Answer in one short sentence:

What does John 1:14 teach you about Jesus?

____

____

____

Jesus Is God With Us!

John 1:14

Jesus came to _______________________________

Jesus lived among us to show _______________________

I can trust Jesus when _______________________

WEEK 19
Love Jesus' Perfect Obedience

"For we do not have a high priest who is unable to empathize with our weaknesses, but we have one who has been tempted in every way, just as we are—yet he did not sin." - Hebrews 4:15

BIG TRUTH: Jesus understands temptation because He faced it, but He never sinned—so He is the perfect Savior who can help you.

WARM-UP: Have you ever wanted to do something wrong even though you knew it was wrong?

That pull inside, when you want to snap, lie, cheat, or be mean, that's temptation. Temptation is not the same as sin. Temptation is the pressure to sin.

Hebrews 4:15 tells us something important: Jesus understands what it feels like to be tempted.

But Jesus also did something nobody else has done:**He never sinned.**

What Hebrews 4:15 Is Saying

This verse teaches two truths at the same time:

1. **Jesus has been tempted as we are.**

   Jesus lived a real human life. He faced pressure, weakness, sadness, and temptation. That means Jesus understands what you go through.

2. **Jesus was "without sin."**

   Jesus never lied. Jesus never disobeyed the Father. Jesus never acted selfishly. Jesus never sinned in His words, actions, or heart.

That's what we mean by "perfect obedience." Jesus always obeyed God.

Why Jesus' Obedience Matters

You might think, "Okay… but why does that matter to me?"

It matters because Jesus didn't come only to teach. He came to rescue.

To rescue sinners, Jesus had to be sinless. If Jesus had sinned even once, He would need rescuing too. But Jesus is the sinless Savior. He is the One who can take our place.

Jesus' perfect obedience is part of God's rescue plan.

Jesus Understands Your Struggle

Sometimes kids feel ashamed to admit temptation.

You might think:

- ✞ "If I tell anyone, they'll think I'm bad."
- ✞ "God must be disappointed with me."
- ✞ "I'm the only one who struggles like this."

Hebrews 4:15 pushes back on that. Jesus understands temptation. He isn't surprised. He is not far away and annoyed. He is near, and He helps.

How Jesus Helps You When You're Tempted

Jesus helps you in at least three ways:

1. **He gives you hope.**

   You are not stuck. Temptation is not your boss.

2. **He gives you a better example.**

   Jesus showed what obedience looks like.

3. **He gives you help.**

   You can pray in the moment. You can ask for strength. You can ask for wisdom.

Temptation often feels strongest when you are tired, hungry, angry, or lonely. In those moments, pause and pray.

A Simple Plan for Temptation

Try this three-step plan:

1. **Stop** - Don't rush into the wrong choice.

2. **Pray** - "Jesus, help me obey."

3. **Choose** - One right step (walk away, tell the truth, ask for help).

Tiny Step to Try This Week

Pick one temptation you face often (anger, lying, jealousy, mean words). Write one sentence you can pray when it shows up: "Jesus, You understand. Help me obey right now."

WORKBOOK ACTIVITIES

1) Verse Copy (Handwriting Practice)

Copy the Bible focus verse:

"For we do not have a high priest who is unable to empathize with our weaknesses, but we have one who has been tempted in every way, just as we are—yet he did not sin."

Hebrews 4:15

Copy it one more time:

____

____

____

2) Fill in the Blanks

"Jesus has been ____

as we are, yet he did not_____________________________________ ."

Word bank:tempted, sin

3) True or False

Circle **True** or **False**.

1. Jesus understands temptation.   **True / False**

2. Temptation is the same thing as sin.   **True / False**

3. Jesus sinned sometimes.   **True / False**

4. Jesus can help me obey God.   **True / False**

4) Temptation or Sin? (Circle One)

1. You feel angry and want to yell, but you pause. **Temptation / Sin**

2. You lie to avoid trouble.   **Temptation / Sin**

3. You feel jealous but pray instead of being
    mean.   **Temptation / Sin**

4. You push someone because you're annoyed.   **Temptation / Sin**

5) Jesus' Obedience (Write It)

Finish the sentences:

✝ Jesus obeyed God when it was

____

____

✝ Jesus obeyed God even when He felt

____

____

✝ Jesus obeyed God because He _________________the Father.

6) My Temptation Plan (Stop–Pray–Choose)

Choose one temptation from the list and fill it in.

Temptations:anger, lying, jealousy, gossip, disrespect, selfishness

My temptation: ____

1. STOPWhen I feel tempted, I will

____

____

____

2. PRAYJesus, help me

____

____

____

3. CHOOSEMy right step will be

____

____

____

7) Scenario Choices (Circle the Best Response)

1. A friend dares you to break a rule.

    A) do it so they like you

    B) say no and choose what is right

2. You want to blame someone else for your mistake.

    A) blame them

    B) tell the truth

3. You feel like teasing someone to look cool.

    A) tease them

    B) use kind words or walk away

8) Prayer Practice

Write a prayer (5–8 lines):

"Jesus, thank You for obeying perfectly.

____

____

Thank You for understanding temptation.

____

____

Please help me when I am tempted to

____

____

Give me strength to choose what is right.

____

____

Amen."

9) Knowledge Check (One-Minute Review)

Answer in one short sentence:

What does Hebrews 4:15 teach you about Jesus?

____

____

____

____

____

____

____

____

Jesus Chose What Was Right!

Hebrews 4:15

Circle the differences.

WEEK 20
Thank Jesus for the Cross

"He himself bore our sins" in his body on the cross, so that we might die to sins and live for righteousness; "by his wounds you have been healed." - 1 Peter 2:24

BIG TRUTH: Jesus took our sin on Himself at the cross so we could be forgiven and learn to live God's way.

WARM-UP: Have you ever tried to carry something too heavy?

Maybe it was a backpack packed with books, a big box, or groceries. You might have thought, "I can't do this alone."

Sin is heavier than it looks. Sin brings guilt, shame, broken trust, and separation from God. You can't fix sin by promising harder or trying to be "good enough."

That's why the cross matters so much. Jesus did what we could not do.

What 1 Peter 2:24 Is Saying

This verse says, "He himself bore our sins..."

"To bear" means to carry. Jesus carried our sins. Not someone else's sins only. Not just "big sins." Our sins, real sins that deserve judgment.

Then it says He bore them "in his body on the tree." "Tree" is another Bible word for the cross.

Jesus didn't rescue us with a speech. He rescued us by taking our place.

The verse also says, "By his wounds you have been healed."

That doesn't mean Christians never get sick. This verse is talking about a deeper healing: healing from sin's greatest damage, being separated from God and trapped in sinful ways.

Why Did Jesus Have to Die?

God is loving, but God is also just. Justice means God does what is right.

Sin is not "oops." Sin is rebellion against the holy God. Sin deserves judgment. If a judge said, "Crime doesn't matter," that would be unfair.

So how can God be both just and forgiving?

This is where the cross shines:

- ✝ God's justice is satisfied because sin is punished.
- ✝ God's mercy is shown because Jesus takes the punishment for sinners who trust Him.

Jesus is the innocent Savior who took the place of guilty people.

What the Cross Shows You About God

The cross shows:

- ✝ God hates sin (because it is truly evil)
- ✝ God loves sinners (because He sent Jesus)
- ✝ God keeps His rescue promise
- ✝ God can forgive completely

The cross is not a symbol of defeat. It is the center of God's rescue plan.

What the Cross Changes for You

If you trust Jesus, the cross means:

- ✝ you can confess sin honestly
- ✝ you don't have to hide in shame
- ✝ you can be forgiven
- ✝ you can begin to change

1 Peter 2:24 also says this rescue leads to a new way of living. Jesus didn't save you so you can keep loving sin. Jesus saves you so you can learn righteousness, living God's way.

Tiny Step to Try This Week

Each day, say a short thank-you prayer: "Jesus, thank You for taking my sin. Help me live Your way today."

WORKBOOK ACTIVITIES

1) Verse Copy (Handwriting Practice)

Copy the Bible focus phrase:

"He himself bore our sins" in his body on the cross, so that we might die to sins and live for righteousness; "by his wounds you have been healed." - **1 Peter 2:24**

Copy it one more time:

____

____

____

____

2) Fill in the Blanks

"He himself bore our _______________________________________

in his body on the _____________________________________ ."

Word bank:sins, cross

3) True or False

Circle **True** or **False**.

1. Jesus carried our sins at the cross.   **True / False**

2. I can fix my sin by trying harder all by myself.   **True / False**

3. The cross shows God's love and God's justice.   **True / False**

4. Jesus saved us so we can keep sinning without care. **True / False**

4) What Does "Bore" Mean? (Circle One)

To "bear" means

      A) to forget

      B) to carry

      C) to laugh

Write one sentence in your own words:

"Jesus bore my sins, which means ________________________________."

5) Cross Truth Match

Draw lines to match.

1. Sin   A) God's rescue plan

2. Cross   B) breaks God's ways

3. Forgiveness   C) God removes guilt for those who trust Jesus

4. Justice   D) God does what is right

6) "Heavy Load" List

Write 3 wrong choices that can feel heavy later (examples: lying, stealing, mean words).

1. ____

2. ____

3. ____

Now write a better truth:

Jesus can forgive me when I confess, so I will

____

____

____

____

____

____

7) Confession and Thanks

Write one honest sentence to God:

God, I'm sorry for

____

____

Now write one thank-you sentence:

Jesus, thank You for

____

____

8) Living God's Way (One Step)

Because Jesus saved you, write one right step you want to practice this week:

This week I want to:

____

____

When I'm tempted, I will:

____

____

9) Prayer Practice

Write a prayer (5–9 lines):

"Jesus, thank You for the cross.

____

____

Thank You for carrying my sin.

____

____

____

Please forgive me for

____

____

Help me turn from sin and live Your way.

____

____

Amen."

10) Knowledge Check (One-Minute Review)

Answer in one short sentence:

What does 1 Peter 2:24 teach you about what Jesus did for you?

____

____

____

Thank You, Jesus!
1 Peter 2:24
He Took My Sin
One thing I want to confess to God:
One thing I thank Jesus for:
One way I want to live differently:

WEEK 21
Celebrate Jesus Alive Again

"He is not here; he has risen, just as he said. Come and see the place where he lay." - Matthew 28:6

Big Truth: Jesus rose from the dead, so sin and death do not win, and everyone who trusts Him has real hope.

Warm-Up: Have you ever had a day that felt like everything went wrong? Maybe you felt sad, disappointed, or scared, and it seemed like nothing could fix it.

The first followers of Jesus had a day like that. Jesus died on the cross, and they thought the story was over.

But Matthew 28 says the story was not over. God's plan was not finished.

What Matthew 28:6 Is Saying

On the third day after Jesus died, some women went to Jesus' tomb. They expected to find a sealed grave and a dead body.

Instead, an angel told them: "He is not here; he has risen, just as he said."

That sentence means:

- ✝ **Jesus was really dead.**
- ✝ **Jesus is really alive.**
- ✝ **Jesus kept His word.** ("as he said")

Jesus didn't rise because people wished hard enough. Jesus rose because God has power over death.

Why the Resurrection Matters

The resurrection is not just an exciting miracle. It's the proof that Jesus is who He says He is.

If Jesus stayed dead, we would have no Savior. But Jesus is alive, which means:

✝ Jesus truly defeated sin's penalty

✝ death does not have the final word

✝ Jesus can forgive and change hearts

✝ Jesus can be trusted

The resurrection is like God's big "Yes!" to Jesus' work on the cross.

"As He Said"

This part is easy to miss, but it's important.

Jesus told His followers ahead of time that He would rise again. When it happened, it proved Jesus tells the truth.

If Jesus kept that promise, you can trust His other promises too.

What This Means for Your Life

Because Jesus is alive:

✝ you are never following a dead hero

✝ you can pray to a living Savior

✝ you can have courage when you feel afraid

✝ you can have hope when life feels sad

✝ you can remember that evil won't win forever

Christians still face hard things. Christians still die someday. But the resurrection means death is not the end. God will make all things new.

How Do We Respond?

The women at the tomb were shocked and joyful. They listened to the angel and went to tell others.

A good response for you is:

- ✝ believe Jesus is alive
- ✝ worship Him
- ✝ tell the truth about Him
- ✝ live with hope

Tiny Step to Try This Week

Each morning this week, say: "Jesus, You are alive. Help me live with hope today."

WORKBOOK ACTIVITIES

1) Verse Copy (Handwriting Practice)

Copy the Bible focus verse:

"He is not here; he has risen, just as he said." - **Matthew 28:6**

Copy it one more time:

____

____

2) Fill in the Blanks

"He is not here, for he has __________________________ ,

just as he ___________________________ ."

Word bank: risen, said

3) True or False

Circle **True** or **False**.

1. Jesus rose from the dead.   **True / False**
2. The resurrection means Jesus keeps His promises.   **True / False**
3. Death wins forever.   **True / False**
4. Christians can have real hope because Jesus is alive.   **True / False**

4) Why It Matters (Match It)

Draw lines to match each truth to what it means.

1. Jesus is alive   A) Jesus can be trusted

2. Jesus kept His word   B) Christians have hope

3. Jesus defeated death   C) we follow a living Savior

5) Hope in Real Life

Write one hard moment you might face (or have faced):

____

Now write one hopeful sentence based on the resurrection:

____

____

Finish this sentence:

"Because Jesus is alive, I can _________________________."

6) Tell the Good News (Short Practice)

Write one sentence you could tell a friend about Easter:

____

Now write a question you could ask:

"Do you know that Jesus _____________________________ ?"

7) Joy and Fear Check

Circle the best answer:

When the women heard Jesus was alive, they probably felt:

   A) nothing
   B) only boredom
   C) shock, joy, and hope

Write one feeling you have when you think about Jesus rising:

____

____

8) **Prayer Practice**

Write a prayer (5–8 lines):

"Jesus, thank You for rising from the dead.

____

____

Thank You for keeping Your promises.

____

____

Help me trust You when I feel

____

____

Help me live with hope and courage today.

____

____

Amen."

9) **Knowledge Check (One-Minute Review)**

Answer in one short sentence:

What does Matthew 28:6 teach you about Jesus?

____

____

____

Empty Tomb "Stone-Roll" Mini Craft (Cut-and-Flap)

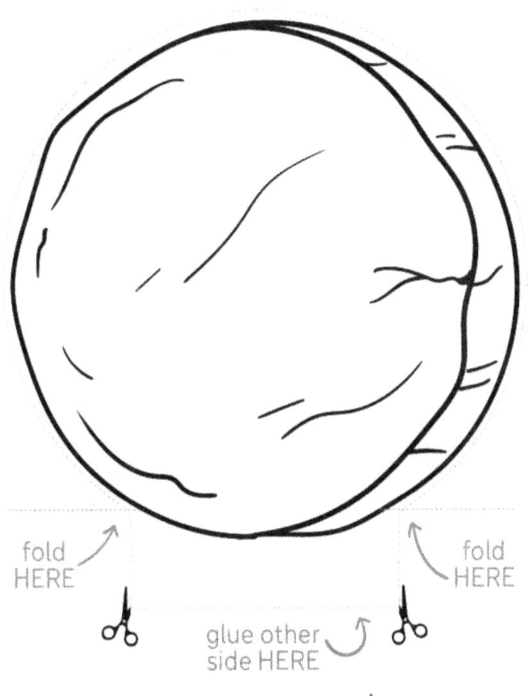
fold
HERE
fold
HERE
glue other
side HERE

WEEK 22
Honor Jesus as Our Priest and King

"Therefore he is able to save completely those who come to God through him, because he always lives to intercede for them." - Hebrews 7:25

BIG TRUTH: Jesus is our perfect Priest and King. He saves completely, and He helps you by praying for you and bringing you near to God.

WARM-UP: Have you ever wanted someone to speak for you?

Maybe you felt nervous to explain something to a teacher. Or you didn't know how to say sorry. Or you needed help asking a question.

It's a relief when someone wise and kind steps in and helps you.

Hebrews 7:25 tells us Jesus does something like that, only bigger and better. Jesus helps people come near to God, and He keeps helping.

What Is a Priest? (Kid-Sized)

In the Bible, a priest was someone who represented people before God. Priests offered sacrifices and prayed for the people.

But those priests were not perfect. They sinned too. They needed help too.

That's why Jesus is such good news. Jesus is the perfect Priest.

What Hebrews 7:25 Is Saying

This verse teaches three powerful truths:

1. **Jesus saves completely.**

   "Therefore he is able to save completely ..."

   This means all the way. Jesus doesn't do half a rescue.

2. **Jesus brings you near to God.**

"...those who come to God through him ...."

You don't come to God by being "good enough." You come through Jesus, trusting Him.

3. **Jesus keeps helping.**

"... because he always lives to intercede for them.."

This means Jesus speaks to the Father for His people. Jesus prays for His people. Jesus is alive, and He is still caring for you.

That's amazing: Jesus doesn't rescue you and then forget you. He keeps helping you.

Jesus Is Also King

A priest represents you. A king rules for you.

Jesus is both.

As King, Jesus:

✞ leads His people

✞ protects His people

✞ rules with goodness and justice

✞ will defeat evil completely in the end

So Jesus is not only a helper. He is the rightful King of your life.

Why This Matters When You Feel Weak

Sometimes kids think, "I prayed, but I still feel scared," or "I messed up again."

This verse brings comfort:

✞ Jesus saves completely.

✞ Jesus is alive.

✞ Jesus is still helping.

✞ Jesus invites you to draw near.

When you feel weak, you don't have to run away from God. You can draw near through Jesus.

How to "Draw Near"

Drawing near can look like:

- ✝ praying honestly
- ✝ confessing sin
- ✝ asking God for help
- ✝ reading Scripture
- ✝ trusting Jesus even when you feel unsure

You're not earning closeness. You're receiving it.

Tiny Step to Try This Week

Once a day, pray this simple prayer:

"Jesus, thank You for saving me. Help me draw near to God today."

WORKBOOK ACTIVITIES

1) Verse Copy (Handwriting Practice)

Copy the Bible focus phrase:

"Therefore he is able to save completely those who come to God through him, because he always lives to intercede for them." - **Hebrews 7:25**

Copy it one more time:

____

____

____

2) Fill in the Blanks

"He is able to _____ completely those who come to God through him."

Write the missing word: _________________________________

3) Word Helper (Match the Meaning)

Draw lines to match.

1. Priest   A) someone who speaks for others

2. King   B) someone who rules

3. Intercession   C) praying and speaking to God for someone

4. Uttermost   D) completely, all the way

4) True or False

Circle **True** or **False**.

1. Jesus saves completely.   **True / False**

2. Jesus is alive and still helps His people.   **True / False**

3. I can come near to God by being perfect.   **True / False**

4. Jesus is both Priest and King.   **True / False**

5) Draw Near Choices (Circle the Best One)

1. You sin and feel guilty.

    A) hide from God

    B) confess and draw near through Jesus

2. You feel nervous.

    A) panic alone

    B) pray and ask Jesus for help

3. You feel unsure about something.

    A) pretend you don't care

    B) read Scripture and ask for wisdom

6) **"Jesus Helps Me" List**

Write five ways Jesus helps you as Priest and King.

1. ____

2. ____

3. ____

4. ____

5. ____

Star the one you need most today: ★

7) **Prayer Starters (Write Your Own)**

Finish these five prayer starters:

1. Jesus, please help me with

____

____

2. Jesus, I'm thankful for

____

____

3. Jesus, please forgive me for

____

____

4. Jesus, help my family with

____

____

5. Jesus, help me follow You when

____

____

8) Prayer Practice

Write a prayer (6–10 lines):

"Jesus, thank You for being my Priest and King.

____

____

Thank You for saving me completely.

____

____

Thank You for helping me draw near to God.

____

____

Please help me with

____

____

Help me follow You today.

____

____

Amen."

9) Knowledge Check (One-Minute Review)

Answer in one short sentence:

What does Hebrews 7:25 teach you about what Jesus is doing right now?

____

____

____

____

____

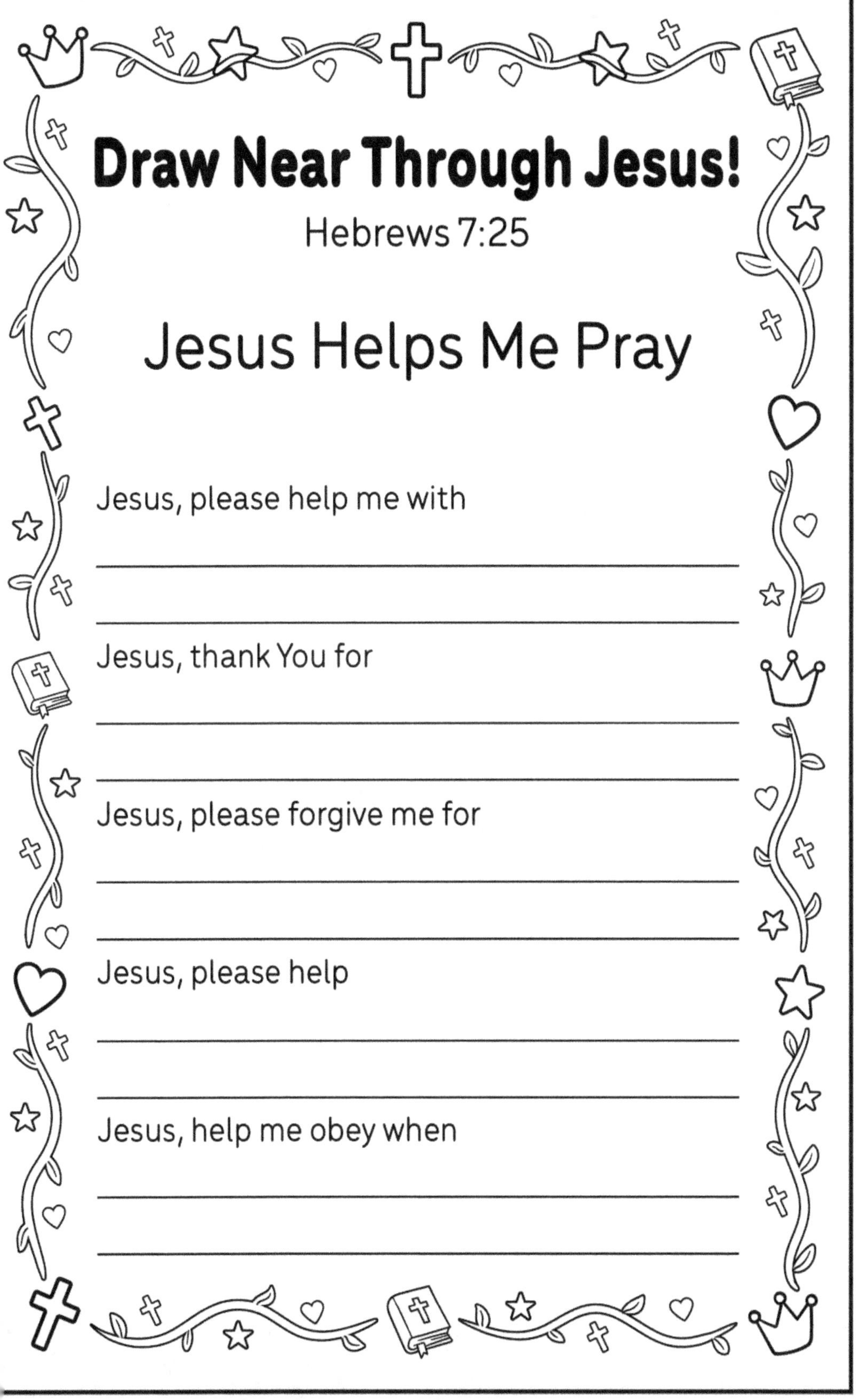

Draw Near Through Jesus!

Hebrews 7:25

Jesus Helps Me Pray

Jesus, please help me with

____

____

Jesus, thank You for

____

____

Jesus, please forgive me for

____

____

Jesus, please help

____

____

Jesus, help me obey when

____

____

PART FIVE
Salvation (God Saves)

WEEK 23
Receive Grace as a Gift

"For it is by grace you have been saved, through faith—and this is not from yourselves, it is the gift of God— not by works, so that no one can boast." - Ephesians 2:8-9

BIG TRUTH: Grace means God saves you as a gift, not because you earned it.

WARM-UP: Have you ever gotten a real gift, one you didn't pay for and didn't work for?

A gift is not the same as a prize. A prize is something you earn by winning or doing a great job. A gift is given because someone wants to give it.

Ephesians 2:8-9 tells us salvation is like a gift. That means God saves people by **grace**.

What Grace Means (Kid Words)

Grace is God's kindness to people who don't deserve it.

That might sound strange at first. We like earning things. We like hearing, "Good job, you deserve it."

But salvation is different.

If salvation depended on being good enough, nobody would make it. We all sin. We all fall short. We all need rescue.

So God gives salvation by grace.

What Ephesians 2:8–9 Is Saying

This verse teaches three main truths:

1. **"By grace you have been saved…"**

   Saved means rescued. God rescues sinners through Jesus.

2. **"…through faith."**

   Faith means trust. You are saved when you trust Jesus—who He is and what He did.

3. **"It is the gift of God, not a result of works."**

   Works are good deeds. The Bible is saying you don't earn salvation by doing enough good things.

That means salvation is not like climbing a ladder to reach God. It's like God coming down to rescue you.

But Do Good Works Matter?

Yes, but not as a way to earn salvation.

Good works are like fruit on a healthy tree. A tree doesn't become alive because it grows fruit. The tree grows fruit because it is alive.

In the same way, Christians obey God because they are saved, not to get saved.

Grace changes your heart so you want to live God's way.

Why Grace Is Such Good News

Grace means you don't have to pretend.

You can:

+ admit your sin

+ confess honestly

+ stop trying to impress God

+ rest in what Jesus has done

Grace also means you don't have to look down on other people. If salvation is a gift, nobody can brag. We can be humble and thankful.

A Kid Picture That Helps

Imagine you fell into a deep hole you can't climb out of. You can jump and try and fail all day.

Then someone lowers a strong rope and pulls you out.

That rescue is like grace. You didn't pull yourself out. You received help you needed.

Jesus is the Savior who rescues. Grace is the way God gives that rescue.

Tiny Step to Try This Week

Every day this week, say:

"God, thank You for grace. Help me trust Jesus and live with gratitude."

WORKBOOK ACTIVITIES

1) Verse Copy (Handwriting Practice)

Copy the Bible focus phrase:

"For it is by grace you have been saved, through faith—and this is not from yourselves, it is the gift of God— not by works, so that no one can boast." **- Ephesians 2:8**

Copy it one more time:

____

____

____

____

2) Fill in the Blanks

"For it is by ____________________ you have been saved, through _________________... it is the _______________________ of God."

Word bank: grace, faith, gift

3) **True or False**

Circle **True** or **False**.

1. Salvation is something I earn by being perfect. **True / False**

2. Grace means God gives kindness we don't deserve. **True / False**

3. Faith means trusting Jesus. **True / False**

4. Christians do good works to show gratitude,
   not to brag. **True / False**

4) **Gift or Prize? (Circle One)**

1. You win a race and get a medal. **Gift / Prize**

2. Someone gives you a birthday present. **Gift / Prize**

3. You clean your room and get an allowance. **Gift / Prize**

4. God saves sinners through Jesus. **Gift / Prize**

Write one sentence:

"Salvation is a gift because ________________________________."

5) **Match the Word to the Meaning**

Draw lines to match.

1. Grace   A) trusting Jesus

2. Faith   B) rescued from sin

3. Saved   C) God's kindness we don't earn

4. Works   D) good deeds

6) **"Not Earned" Check**

Circle what you *can't* use to earn salvation:

✟ being kind sometimes

✟ getting good grades

✟ going to church

✟ never making mistakes

✟ doing chores

✟ **(Answernone of these can earn salvation.)**

Now write this truth in your own words:

"I can't earn salvation by ______________________________________

I receive salvation by trusting______________________________________

______________________________________ ."

7) Thankful Heart List

Write 5 things you can thank God for because of grace:

1. ______________________________________

2. ______________________________________

3. ______________________________________

4. ______________________________________

5. ______________________________________

8) Prayer Practice

Write a prayer (6–10 lines):

"God, thank You for saving by grace.

____

____

Thank You that salvation is a gift.

____

____

Please help me trust Jesus more.

____

____

Help me obey You because I'm thankful, not because I'm trying to earn Your love.

____

____

Amen."

9) **Knowledge Check (One-Minute Review)**

Answer in one short sentence:

What do Ephesians 2:8–9 teach you about grace?

9) **Knowledge Check (One-Minute Review)**

Answer in one short sentence:

What do Ephesians 2:8–9 teach you about grace?

Color the gift

Grace = Gift

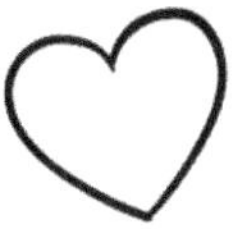

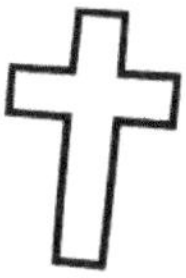

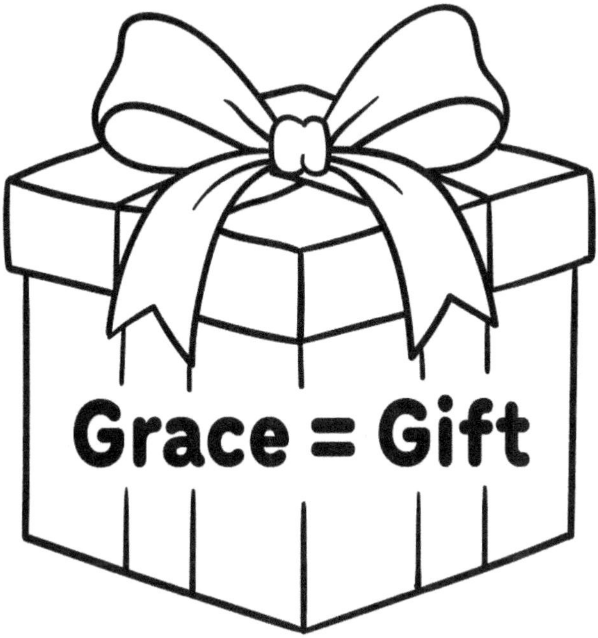

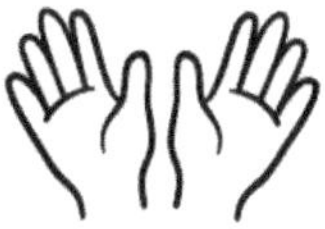

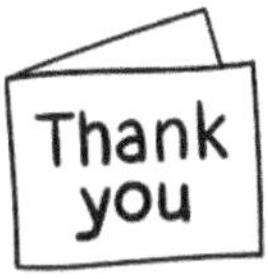

Section A: *Gift-Box Coloring*

Draw lines to match the truth.

**Things I might try to
earn God's love**

**What
the Bible says**

| Being perfect | Salvation is a gift |

| Doing chores | Grace, not works |

| Getting good grades | Trust Jesus |

| Never messing up | God forgives |

| Being better than others | No one can brag |

Ephesians 2:8–9

WEEK 24
Repent and Return to God

"Repent, then, and turn to God, so that your sins may be wiped out, that times of refreshing may come from the Lord," - Acts 3:19

BIG TRUTH: Repentance means turning away from sin and turning back to God.

WARM-UP: Have you ever walked the wrong way and then realized it?

Maybe you followed the wrong hallway at school. Maybe you went the wrong direction in a store. When you notice, you don't just keep going and hope it works out. You turn around.

Acts 3:19 uses that same idea for your heart and your life.

What Acts 3:19 Is Saying

This verse says: "Repent, then, and turn to God,..."

Repentance is not only feeling bad. Feeling bad is part of it sometimes, but repentance is bigger.

Repentance means:

✝ you admit your sin

✝ you agree with God that it is wrong

✝ you turn away from it

✝ you turn back to God

The verse also says, "so that your sins may be wiped out."

God does not forgive in a half way. God forgives fully when sinners come to Him.

What Repentance Is NOT

Repentance is not:

- ✟ saying "sorry" but doing the same thing again on purpose
- ✟ blaming others
- ✟ making excuses
- ✟ hiding your sin
- ✟ trying to pay God back

You can't pay God back for forgiveness. Forgiveness is grace.

Repentance is the honest turning of your heart toward God.

Why God Calls Us to Repent

God calls people to repent because sin harms us.

Sin can feel good for a moment, but it always lies. It promises happiness and delivers trouble.

Repentance is God's kindness. It's like God saying, "Come back. This is not the way."

A Kid Picture That Helps

Think of a "U-turn" sign on the road.

A U-turn sign isn't trying to ruin your day. It's trying to keep you from getting lost or driving into danger.

Repentance is a heart U-turn:

- ✟ away from sin
- ✟ back to God

What Turning Back Looks Like in Real Life

Repentance can include actions, not just words.

If you lied, turning back may mean telling the truth.

If you were mean, turning back may mean apologizing.

If you stole, turning back may mean returning it.

If you kept gossiping, turning back may mean stopping and making peace.

You won't fix everything perfectly overnight. But repentance is real when you truly turn and start walking a new direction with God's help.

God Welcomes Repentant Sinners

Some kids think, "If God knew what I did, He wouldn't want me."

But God already knows. And He still invites you to repent and return.

God is not waiting to crush you. God is ready to forgive and help you grow.

Tiny Step to Try This Week

When you notice sin, practice this simple prayer: "God, I confess this sin. Please forgive me. Help me turn back to You."

WORKBOOK ACTIVITIES

1) Verse Copy (Handwriting Practice)

Copy the Bible focus verse:

"Repent, then, and turn to God, so that your sins may be wiped out, that times of refreshing may come from the Lord," - **Acts 3:19**

Copy it one more time:

____

____

____

____

2) Fill in the Blanks

"_____________________, then, and ______________ to God..."

Write the two missing words: ______________________________

3) True or False

Circle **True** or **False**.

1. Repentance is only feeling sad.   **True / False**

2. Repentance includes turning away from sin.   **True / False**

3. God can forgive sins when we repent.   **True / False**

4. Turning back to God means we run toward Him,
   not away.   **True / False**

4) Match the Word to the Meaning

Draw lines to match.

1. Repent   A) wiped away

2. Turn to   B) change direction and return to God

3. Wiped out   C) stop going the wrong way and go back

5) Turn From / Turn To (Write It)

Fill in the chart with your own examples.

Turn from:(sin / wrong choice)

____

____

Turn to:(right choice / God's way)

____

____

6) What Should I Do Next? (Circle the Best Answer)

1. You lied.

     A) keep lying

     B) tell the truth and ask forgiveness

2. You hurt someone's feelings.

     A) ignore it

     B) apologize and make peace

3. You disobeyed and got caught.

   A) blame someone else

   B) confess and accept correction

4. You keep getting angry fast.

   A) say "that's just me"

   B) ask God for help and practice self-control

7) Repentance Prayer Practice

Write a short prayer (5–8 lines):

"God, I repent of

____

____

I don't want to keep walking that way.

____

____

Please forgive me and blot out my sin.

____

____

Help me turn back to You and choose

____

____

Amen."

8) One Step Back to God

Write one action step you can take today:

Today I will turn back by _______________________

____

____

____

Knowledge Check (One-Minute Review)

Answer in one short sentence:

What does Acts 3:19 teach you to do when you sin?

____

____

____

Make a Heart U-Turn!

TURN FROM	TURN TO
Lying	Truth
Disobeying	Obeying
Unkind words	Kind words
Selfishness	Sharing
Anger	Peace
Cheating	Honesty
Hitting	Gentleness
Pride	Humility

Acts 3:19

WEEK 25
Trust Jesus (Faith)

"Now faith is confidence in what we hope for and assurance about what we do not see." - Hebrews 11:1

BIG TRUTH: Faith means trusting God's promises and trusting Jesus, even when you can't see everything clearly yet.

WARM-UP: Have you ever trusted someone enough to follow them, even when you didn't know the whole plan?

Maybe a parent said, "Hold my hand," and you did. Maybe a coach said, "Try it this way," and you listened. Maybe a teacher said, "I'll help you," and you believed them.

That kind of trust gives you a picture of faith, but faith in God is even stronger, because God never lies.

What Hebrews 11:1 Is Saying

This verse uses two words to explain faith:

✝ **Assurance of things hoped for**

✝ **Conviction of things not seen**

Let's break those down.

Hope in the Bible is not the same as "I hope I get candy." Bible hope is a confident hope. It means you are expecting God to keep His promises.

Assurance means you have a firm foundation. It's like standing on solid ground.

Conviction means you are convinced something is true.

So faith means you trust what God says is true—even when you can't see everything with your eyes.

Faith Is Not Pretending

Faith is not closing your eyes and making things up.

Faith is trusting the real God who has shown Himself:

- ✟ through creation
- ✟ through Scripture
- ✟ through Jesus' life, death, and resurrection
- ✟ through God's faithfulness to His people through history

Faith has reasons. Faith is not foolish.

Why Faith Matters for Salvation

You are not saved by being "good enough." You are saved by grace through faith.

Faith is like reaching out your hand to take the gift God offers in Jesus.

Faith says: "Jesus, I believe You are the Savior. I trust You."

Faith and Feelings

Sometimes people think faith means you always feel brave and happy.

But feelings change. Some days you might feel strong. Some days you might feel shaky.

Faith is choosing to trust God even when feelings wobble.

You can say: "God, I believe. Please help me when I struggle."

A Kid Picture That Helps

Imagine you're wearing glasses. The glasses don't create the world. The glasses help you see what is already there.

Faith doesn't create God. Faith helps you see the truth and respond to it.

Faith also helps you walk forward when you don't know every detail. It's like using a flashlight at night. The light doesn't show the whole road, but it shows the next step.

Ways to Grow Your Faith

Faith can grow.

Here are three ways:

1. **Read God's Word** (faith feeds on truth)

2. **Pray honestly** (tell God what you feel)

3. **Obey in small steps** (trust grows when you practice it)

Tiny Step to Try This Week

Choose one promise of God (like "God is with you" or "God forgives"). Write it down and read it every day this week. Then pray: "God, help me trust You."

WORKBOOK ACTIVITIES

1) Verse Copy (Handwriting Practice)

Copy the Bible focus verse:

"Now faith is confidence in what we hope for and assurance about what we do not see." - **Hebrews 11:1**

Copy it one more time:

____

____

2) Fill in the Blanks

"Now faith is _______________________________in what we

hope for and _____________________ about what we do not see."

Word bank: assurance, confidence

3) Match the Word to the Meaning

Draw lines to match.

1. Faith   A) confident trust in God

2. Assurance   B) firm foundation / certainty

3. Conviction   C) being convinced something is true

4. Hope   D) confident waiting for God to keep promises

4) **True or False**

Circle **True** or **False**.

1. Faith is pretending something is true. **True / False**

2. Faith means trusting God even when I can't
    see everything. **True / False**

3. Faith is the same as never having questions. **True / False**

4. Faith grows when I learn God's Word and obey. **True / False**

5) **Faith or Not Faith? (Circle One)**

1. "I will trust God's promise even when I'm
    nervous." **Faith / Not faith**

2. "I'll only trust God if I get what I want
    today." **Faith / Not faith**

3. "Jesus rose from the dead, so I can trust
    Him." **Faith / Not faith**

4. "God can't help me because I can't see
    Him." **Faith / Not faith**

6) **What Do I Hope For? (Bible Hope)**

Write one promise you can trust God to keep:

God promises

____

____

Now write one sentence:

"I have faith because God is ___________________________

____

____

7) **My Faith Steps**

Write one "next step" you can take in faith this week:

At school, I can trust God by

____

____

At home, I can trust God by

____

____

With friends, I can trust God by

____

____

8) **Prayer Practice**

Write a prayer (6–10 lines):

"God, thank You that You tell the truth.

____

____

Help me trust You even when I can't see everything.

____

____

Help me have assurance and conviction.

____

____

Help me trust Jesus as my Savior.

____

____

Amen."

 Knowledge Check (One-Minute Review)

Answer in one short sentence:

What does Hebrews 11:1 teach you about faith?

____

____

____

Hebrews 11:1

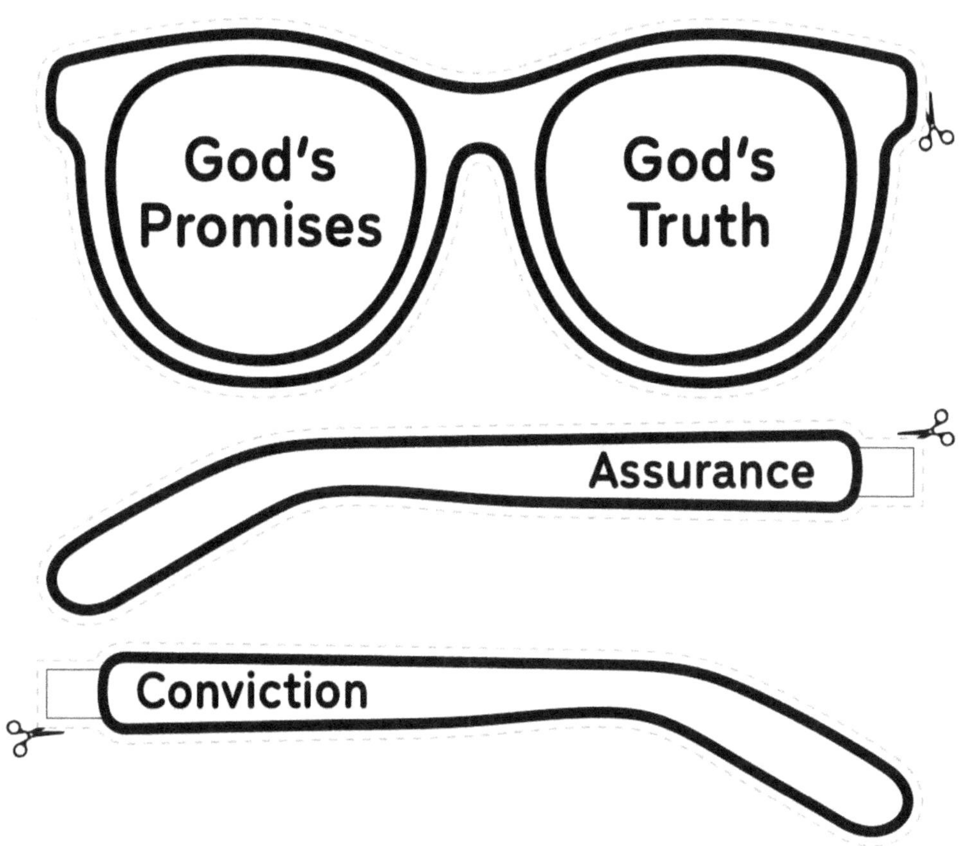

God is with me.

God forgives.

Jesus is alive.

God helps me obey.

WEEK 26
Celebrate Being Made New

"Therefore, if anyone is in Christ, the new creation has come: The old has gone, the new is here!" - 2 Corinthians 5:17

BIG TRUTH: When you belong to Jesus, God changes you from the inside out. You are a new creation.

WARM-UP: Have you ever watched something get turned into something new?

Maybe you saw:

- ✝ a messy room become clean
- ✝ a broken toy get fixed
- ✝ old ingredients become cookies
- ✝ a plain drawing become colorful

Change can be exciting. But the change God does is even better. God doesn't only clean up the outside. God makes something new on the inside.

That's what 2 Corinthians 5:17 is talking about.

What 2 Corinthians 5:17 Is Saying

This verse begins: "Therefore, if anyone is in Christ, the new creation has come: The old has gone, the new is here!"

"In Christ" means you belong to Jesus. You trust Him as Savior and follow Him as Lord.

Then it says, "the new creation."

That means God gives you new life. You are not the same person you were before. You may still have struggles, but God is at work changing you.

The verse also says, "The old has gone, the new is here!"

This doesn't mean your old temptations disappear overnight. It means your old life, your life ruled by sin, doesn't have to be your boss anymore.

What Changes When God Makes You New

Here are some real changes God begins in His children:

✟ **New heart** You start wanting what is right more than before.

✟ **New direction** You begin turning away from sin and toward God.

✟ **New help** God gives His Spirit to help you grow.

✟ **New identity** You are God's child, not a "hopeless sinner."

✟ **New hope** You are not stuck in the same patterns forever.

Becoming a new creation is not about becoming perfect in one week. It is about becoming new in Christ and growing over time.

Growth Takes Time

Think about a seed. It becomes a plant, but not in one day. It needs water, sunlight, and time.

God grows His children too. He uses:

✟ His Word

✟ prayer

✟ wise people in your life

✟ obedience in small steps

✟ confession and repentance when you mess up

Even when you struggle, God is still working.

A Kid Picture That Helps

Imagine you get a brand-new team jersey. You're part of the team now. You don't play perfectly right away, but you practice and grow because you belong.

Being "in Christ" means you belong to Jesus. And because you belong, God is changing you.

What If You Mess Up Again?

Kids sometimes think, "If I'm a new creation, why do I still sin sometimes?"

Being a new creation doesn't mean you never struggle. It means you now have:

- ✝ forgiveness when you confess
- ✝ power to change
- ✝ a new direction
- ✝ a Savior who helps

When you mess up, you don't quit. You confess and keep following Jesus.

Tiny Step to Try This Week

Choose one "new creation" habit to practice daily this week:

- ✝ pray before you react
- ✝ tell the truth quickly
- ✝ ask forgiveness when you sin
- ✝ read one Bible verse a day
- ✝ Then thank God "Jesus, thank You for making me new."

WORKBOOK ACTIVITIES

1) Verse Copy (Handwriting Practice)

Copy the Bible focus verse:

"Therefore, if anyone is in Christ, the new creation has come: The old has gone, the new is here!" - **2 Corinthians 5:17**

Copy it one more time:

____

____

2) Fill in the Blanks

"If anyone is in _________________________________ ,

the new _________________________________ has come."

Word bank: Christ, creation

3) True or False

Circle **True** or **False**.

1. God only changes the outside of a person. **True / False**
2. Being "in Christ" means belonging to Jesus. **True / False**
3. A new creation means God begins real change in me. **True / False**
4. If I mess up, I should give up on following Jesus. **True / False**

4) Old and New (Match It)

Draw lines to match the "old" habit to a "new" habit.

1. Lying   A) telling the truth
2. Holding a grudge   B) forgiving
3. Being cruel   C) using kind words
4. Being selfish   D) sharing
5. Quitting   E) asking for help and trying again

5) Before and After (Write It)

Write one "old" habit you want to leave behind:

Old: _________________________________

Write one "new" habit God can help you grow:

New: _________________________________

Finish the sentence:

"Jesus is making me new, so I will _________________________________."

6) New Creation Choices (Circle the Best One)

1. You feel tempted to gossip.

    A) join in

    B) stop and choose kind words

2. You feel angry fast.

> A) yell

> B) pause, pray, and speak calmly

3. You lied and feel guilty.

> A) hide

> B) confess and tell the truth

4. You feel like you can't change.

> A) give up

> B) ask God for help and take one small step

7) My Growth Plan

Circle one "new creation" habit to practice this week:

> A) pray daily

> B) read one verse daily

> C) apologize quickly

> D) obey with a good attitude

> E) be kind to someone hard to love

Write your choice: _______________________________________

Now write when you'll practice it:

____

____

8) Prayer Practice

Write a prayer (6–10 lines):

"God, thank You for making new creations in Christ.

____

____

Please change my heart.

____

____

Help me turn away from____ .

Help me grow in ____ .

When I mess up, help me confess and keep following You.

____

____

Amen."

9) **Knowledge Check (One-Minute Review)**

Answer in one short sentence:

What does 2 Corinthians 5:17 teach you about someone who is in Christ?

____

____

____

New Creation!

2 Corinthians 5:17

Before (Old Ways) ✝ After (New Ways)

Before (Old Ways)	After (New Ways)
I lie	I tell the truth"
I get revenge	I forgive
I complain	I'm thankful
I quit	I keep trying
I'm selfish	I share
I disobey	I obey

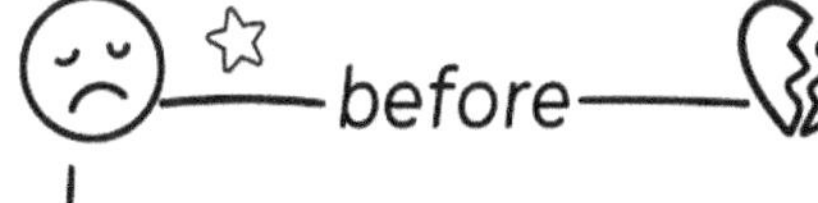

— before —

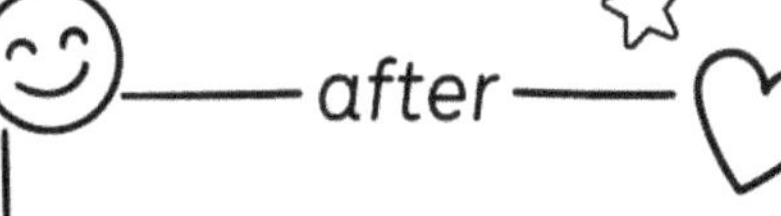

— after —

Use stickers or draw symbols.

WEEK 27
Rejoice in Being God's Child

"Yet to all who did receive him, to those who believed in his name, he gave the right to become children of God—" - John 1:12

BIG TRUTH: When you receive Jesus and believe in Him, God welcomes you into His family as His child.

WARM-UP: Think about what it feels like to belong.

Belonging feels like:

- ✞ you're wanted
- ✞ you're safe
- ✞ you're not alone
- ✞ you have a place

John 1:12 gives one of the happiest truths in the Bible: God doesn't only forgive sinners, He brings them into His family.

What John 1:12 Is Saying

This verse says, "To all who did receive him..."

To "receive" Jesus means you welcome Him. You don't push Him away. You don't treat Him like He doesn't matter. You trust Him.

Then it says, "who believed in his name..."

Believing in Jesus' name means you trust who Jesus is, God's Son, Savior, Lord, and you trust what He did for you.

Then it says something amazing: "He gave the right to become children of God."

That means when you trust Jesus, God gives you a new family name. You belong to Him.

What It Means to Be God's Child

Being God's child does not mean you become a little god. It means you belong to God in a close relationship.

As God's child, you can say:

✝ God loves me

✝ God listens when I pray

✝ God forgives me when I confess

✝ God teaches me

✝ God corrects me for my good

✝ God will never forget me

Being God's child is not something you earn. It is a gift God gives to those who receive Jesus.

Rights and Belonging

The verse says "the right" to become children of God.

A right is something you are allowed to have.

So if you're God's child, you have the right to:

✝ come to God in prayer

✝ ask for help

✝ read God's Word and expect Him to teach you

✝ trust God's promises

✝ live with hope

You don't have to act like a stranger.

God's Family Changes How You Live

When you know you belong to God, it changes your daily life.

You don't have to chase approval like it's your oxygen. You don't have to prove your worth with your grades or your skills. You can obey God not because you're trying to earn love, but because you already have it.

You can also treat other Christians like family. That doesn't mean everyone is your best friend. It means you show love, respect, and forgiveness as part of God's household.

What If My Family Life Is Hard?

Some kids have warm homes. Some kids have hard homes. John 1:12 does not pretend every family is perfect.

But it gives hope: God is a perfect Father, and His love is steady. If you trust Jesus, God welcomes you as His child, and no one can take that away.

Tiny Step to Try This Week

Every day this week, pray one sentence: "Father God, thank You that I belong to You. Help me live like Your child today."

WORKBOOK ACTIVITIES

1) Verse Copy (Handwriting Practice)

Copy the Bible focus verse:

"Yet to all who did receive him, to those who believed in his name, he gave the right to become children of God—" - **John 1:12**

Copy it one more time:

____

____

____

____

2) Fill in the Blanks

"He gave the right to become _______________________________

of ____ ."

Write the missing words: _______________________________

3) True or False

Circle **True** or **False**.

1. I become God's child by earning it with good works. **True / False**

2. Receiving Jesus means welcoming and trusting Him. **True / False**

3. God's children can talk to Him in prayer. **True / False**

4. Being God's child means God will never care about me. **True / False**

4) Receive and Believe (Match It)

Draw lines to match each phrase to what it means.

1. Receive Jesus   A) trust who Jesus is and what He did

2. Believe in His name   B) welcome Jesus as Savior and Lord

3. Children of God   C) belong to God's family

5) God's Child Identity Statements

Circle the statements that are true for God's child:

✝ God hears me when I pray.

✝ God forgets me when I fail.

✝ God loves me with steady love.

✝ I can never come back after I sin.

✝ God forgives when I confess.

✝ I belong to God's family.

6) Family Resemblance (How God's Kids Act)

Write one example for each.

1. God's children show love by

   ____

2. God's children tell the truth by

   ____

3. God's children forgive by

____

4. God's children pray by

____

7) **"I Belong" List**

Write 5 ways belonging to God helps you:

1. ____

2. ____

3. ____

4. ____

5. ____

Star the one you need most today: ★

8) **Prayer Practice**

Write a prayer (6–10 lines):

"Father God, thank You for welcoming me.

____

____

Thank You for giving me the right to become Your child.

____

____

Help me trust Jesus more.

____

____

Help me live like Your child at

____

____

Amen."

9) **Knowledge Check (One-Minute Review)**

9) **Knowledge Check (One-Minute Review)**

Answer in one short sentence:

What does John 1:12 say happens when you receive Jesus and believe in Him?

____

____

____

Welcome to God's Family!
Name:
Today I rejoice that I am a child of God through Jesus.
Signature:
Date:
But to all who did receive him, to those who believed in his name, he gave the right to become children of God
John 1:12

WEEK 28
Rest in God's Love

"For I am convinced that neither death nor life, neither angels nor demons, neither the present nor the future, nor any powers, neither height nor depth, nor anything else in all creation, will be able to separate us from the love of God that is in Christ Jesus our Lord." -
Romans 8:38–39

BIG TRUTH: God's love for His people in Christ is steady, strong, and unbreakable.

WARM-UP: Have you ever worried that someone might stop loving you?

Kids can worry about that for lots of reasons:

- ✞ they messed up
- ✞ they had a bad day
- ✞ they felt left out
- ✞ they heard an angry voice
- ✞ they felt like they weren't "good enough"

Romans 8:38–39 speaks straight into those fears with a strong promise.

What Romans 8:38–39 Is Saying

Paul (the writer) says he is sure, convinced, that nothing can separate God's people from God's love in Christ.

Then he lists a bunch of scary-sounding things:

- ✝ death and life
- ✝ angels and rulers
- ✝ things present and things to come
- ✝ powers
- ✝ height and depth
- ✝ anything else in all creation

That is Paul's way of saying: **nothing in the whole universe is stronger than God's love for His children in Jesus.**

Important This Promise Is "In Christ"

The verse says "the love of God in Christ Jesus our Lord."

That means this promise belongs to people who belong to Jesus, people who trust Him.

God's love is real and kind toward all His creation, but Romans 8 is talking about God's special saving love for His children.

So if you're in Christ, this love is for you.

What "Separate" Means

To separate means to pull apart, to divide, to tear away.

Romans 8 says no one and nothing can pull you out of God's loving grip.

Not:

- ✝ a hard day
- ✝ a scary thought
- ✝ a big change in life
- ✝ a mistake you made
- ✝ people who dislike you
- ✝ your own weakness

This does not mean sin is okay. Sin is still serious. But it means when God saves you, He doesn't toss you away every time you stumble. God is faithful.

Resting Doesn't Mean Doing Nothing

Resting in God's love does not mean:

- ✠ "I don't need to obey"
- ✠ "I don't need to confess sin"
- ✠ "I can do whatever I want"

Resting means you stop trying to earn God's love. You stop living like God's love is a paycheck.

Instead, you live like a child who is safe in the love of a good Father.

Then you obey from gratitude, not fear.

A Kid Picture That Helps

Think of a seatbelt in a car. A good seatbelt holds you tight, even when the road is bumpy.

God's love is stronger than a seatbelt. It holds God's children through hard times, big feelings, and changes in life.

How to Rest in God's Love

Here are three simple ways:

1. **Remember the promise.** Read Romans 8:38–39 again.
2. **Pray honestly.** "God, help me believe Your love is steady."
3. **Take the next right step.** Love doesn't make you lazy. Love makes you secure.

Tiny Step to Try This Week

When you feel worried this week, place your hand over your heart and whisper: "Nothing can separate me from God's love in Christ."

WORKBOOK ACTIVITIES

1) Verse Copy (Handwriting Practice)

Copy the Bible focus phrase:

"For I am convinced that neither death nor life, neither angels nor demons, neither the present nor the future, nor any powers, neither height nor depth, nor anything else in all creation, will be able to separate us from the love of God that is in Christ Jesus our Lord." **Romans 8:38–39**

Copy it one more time:

____

____

____

____

____

____

____

2) Fill in the Blanks

"Nothing will be able to __________________________ us from

the __________________________ of God in Christ Jesus."

Word bank: separate, love

3) True or False

Circle **True** or **False**.

1. God's love changes every time I mess up. **True / False**

2. Romans 8 says nothing can separate God's children from His love in Christ. **True / False**

3. Resting in God's love means I never obey.   **True / False**

4. God's love is stronger than my fears.   **True / False**

4) What Can't Separate? (Circle the True Statements)

Circle the statements that match Romans 8:38–39.

✞ A scary day can separate me from God's love.

✞ God's love in Christ is stronger than life changes.

✞ My weakness is bigger than God's love.

✞ Nothing in creation can separate God's children from His love.

✞ God stops loving His people when they stumble.

✞ God's love is steady in Christ.

5) Worry to Rest (Write It)

Write one worry you have:

____

____

Now write a "rest sentence" you can say when you worry:

____

____

Example: "God's love is steady, and He is with me."

6) God's Love Shield (Fill It In)

Finish the sentences:

✞ When I feel afraid, God's love helps me_______________ .

✞ When I feel guilty, God's love helps me _______________ .

✞ When I feel alone, God's love helps me _______________ .

7) Real-Life Choices (Circle the Best Response)

1. You sinned and feel ashamed.

    A) hide from God

    B) confess and trust God's love

2. You feel nervous about tomorrow.

   A) worry all night

   B) pray and remember God's promise

3. Someone is mean to you.

   A) get revenge

   B) remember God's love and choose what is right

8) **Prayer Practice**

Write a prayer (6–10 lines):

"God, thank You for Your love in Christ Jesus.

____

____

Help me believe Your promise when I feel

____

____

Help me rest instead of panic.

____

____

Help me obey You because I am loved.

____

____

Amen."

9) **Knowledge Check (One-Minute Review)**

Answer in one short sentence:

What do Romans 8:38–39 promise to God's people in Christ?

____

____

____

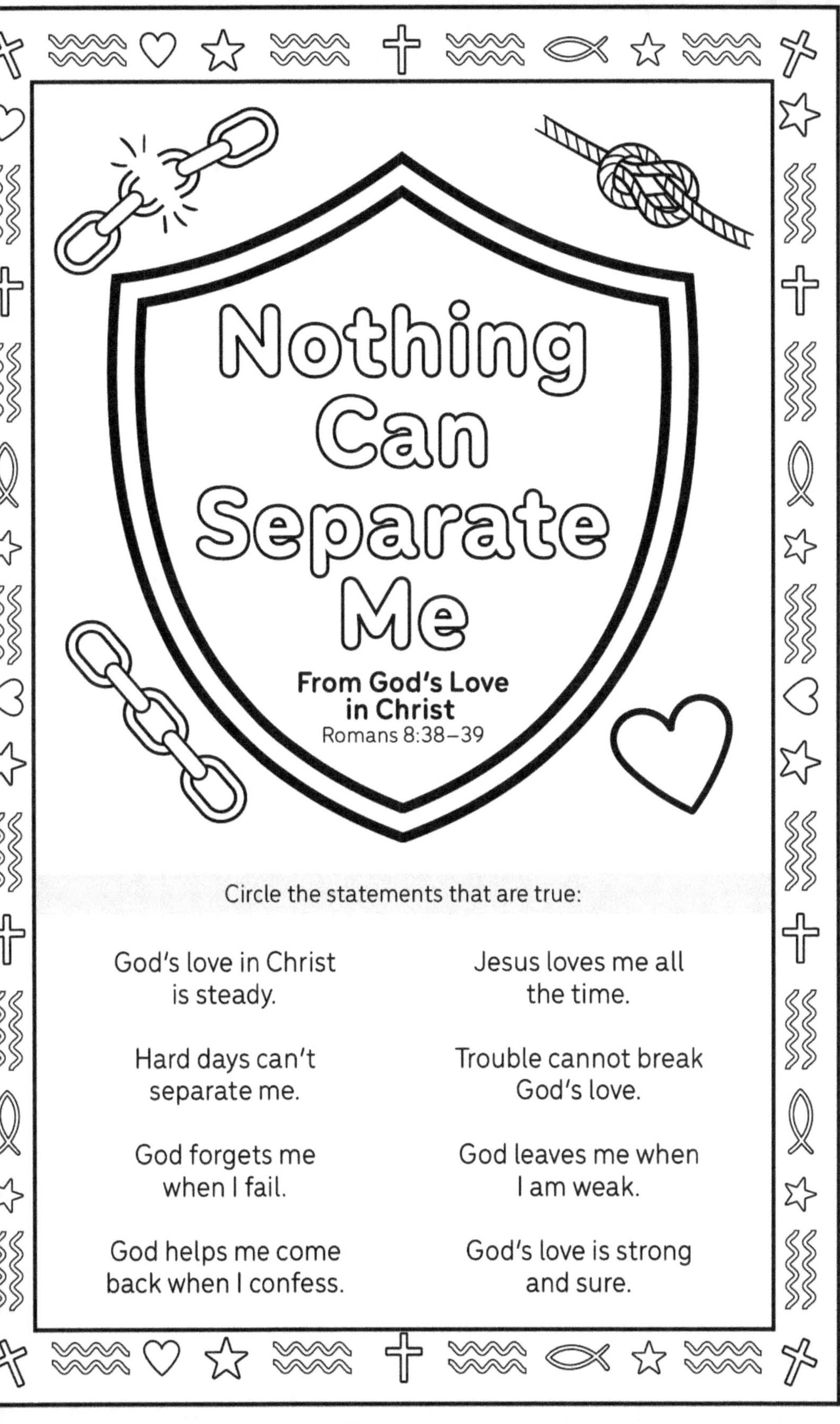

Nothing Can Separate Me
From God's Love in Christ
Romans 8:38–39

Circle the statements that are true:

God's love in Christ is steady.

Jesus loves me all the time.

Hard days can't separate me.

Trouble cannot break God's love.

God forgets me when I fail.

God leaves me when I am weak.

God helps me come back when I confess.

God's love is strong and sure.

PART SIX
The Holy Spirit

WEEK 29
Welcome the Spirit's Help

"But the Advocate, the Holy Spirit, whom the Father will send in my name, will teach you all things and will remind you of everything I have said to you." - John 14:26

BIG TRUTH: The Holy Spirit is God's Helper who teaches God's people and reminds them of Jesus' words.

WARM-UP: **HAVE YOU** ever tried to do something hard all by yourself, then felt relieved when someone helped?

Maybe it was:

✞ a tough homework problem

✞ learning a new skill

✞ cleaning a messy room

✞ making peace after an argument

Jesus knew His followers would need help too. So He promised they would not be alone.

That's where John 14:26 comes in.

What John 14:26 Is Saying

Jesus calls the Holy Spirit **"the Advocate."** That is a wonderful name. It means the Spirit is not distant or uninterested. The Spirit helps God's people.

Jesus also says the Holy Spirit will do two important things:

1. **Teach you**

    The Spirit helps you understand God's truth. This doesn't mean you suddenly know everything. It means God helps His children learn.

2. **Remind you**

    The Spirit brings Jesus' words back to your mind. Sometimes you'll be in a moment where you need wisdom, courage, or comfort. God can bring the right truth to your memory.

Who Is the Holy Spirit?

The Holy Spirit is not a force like electricity. The Holy Spirit is God.

Christians believe God is one God in three Persons: Father, Son, and Holy Spirit. We don't fully understand everything about God, but we can trust what the Bible teaches.

The Holy Spirit:

✤ loves what is right

✤ helps God's people

✤ guides them toward truth

✤ strengthens them to obey

How the Holy Spirit Helps Kids (Real-Life)

Sometimes kids think the Holy Spirit is only for adults. Not true.

The Spirit can help you:

✤ pause before you speak in anger

✤ remember a Bible verse when you feel worried

✤ feel convicted when you sin (so you confess and return)

✤ choose kindness when teasing feels easier

✤ pray when you don't know what to say

The Spirit's help is not loud and showy. Often it feels like a quiet nudge toward what is right.

The Spirit Helps You Learn Jesus' Words

Notice what Jesus says: the Spirit brings to remembrance "all that I have said to you."

That means it helps to put Jesus' words into your mind in the first place.

If you never read Scripture, you're like someone who wants to remember the instructions without ever looking at them.

So a wise plan is:

- ✝ read God's Word
- ✝ listen carefully
- ✝ ask God for help
- ✝ practice obedience

A Kid Picture That Helps

Think of a coach who teaches and reminds.

A good coach says:

- ✝ "Here's what to do." (teaches)
- ✝ "Remember your form." (reminds)

The Holy Spirit does something like that for God's children, only better, because God changes hearts, not just habits.

Tiny Step to Try This Week

Before you read the Bible this week, pray: "Holy Spirit, please help me understand God's Word and remember it."

WORKBOOK ACTIVITIES

1) **Verse Copy (Handwriting Practice)**

Copy the Bible focus phrase:

"But the Advocate, the Holy Spirit, whom the Father will send in my name, will teach you all things and will remind you of everything I have said to you." - **John 14:26**

Copy it one more time:

____

____

____

____

2) **Fill in the Blanks**

"But the ____________________, the Holy______________________

will ____ you all things ..."

Word bank: Advocate Spirit, teach

3) **Word Helper (Match the Meaning)**

Draw lines to match.

1. Helper	A) brings back to your mind
2. Teach	B) someone who gives help
3. Remind	C) helps you understand and learn

4) **True or False**

Circle **True** or **False**.

1. The Holy Spirit is called the Helper.	**True / False**
2. The Holy Spirit can help me understand God's Word.	**True / False**
3. The Holy Spirit only helps adults.	**True / False**
4. The Holy Spirit can remind me of Jesus' words.	**True / False**

5) **What Help Do I Need?**

Circle two areas where you want God's help this week:

- ✝ being patient
- ✝ telling the truth
- ✝ being kind
- ✝ praying
- ✝ obeying quickly
- ✝ not worrying so much
- ✝ forgiving
- ✝ speaking respectfully

Now write one sentence:

"Holy Spirit, please help me with _______________________________

___________________________________ ."

6) **Teach or Remind? (Circle One)**

1. You read a verse and start to understand it better.

Teach / Remind

2. You're about to lie, and a Bible truth pops into your mind.

Teach / Remind

3. You don't know what to pray, and you remember God is near.

Teach / Remind

4. You learn why Jesus came to save sinners.

Teach / Remind

7) **"Helper" Moments (Write It)**

Finish the sentences:

- ✝ When I feel angry, the Holy Spirit can help me

____

____

✝ When I feel nervous, the Holy Spirit can help me

____

✝ When I sin, the Holy Spirit can help me

____

✝ When I read the Bible, the Holy Spirit can help me

____

8) Prayer Practice

Write a prayer (6–10 lines):

"Holy Spirit, thank You for helping God's people.

____

____

Please teach me God's truth.

____

____

Please remind me of Jesus' words when I need them.

____

____

Help me obey God today at

____

____

Amen."

9) Knowledge Check (One-Minute Review)

Answer in one short sentence:

What does John 14:26 teach you about what the Holy Spirit does?

____

____

____

The Helper Is With Me!

John 14:26

Helps me understand a verse

Brings a verse back to my mind

Shows me what is right

Riminds me of God's Word

Helps me remember to pray

Helps me know what Jesus said

Helps me know what Jesus said

Helps me understand God's truth

Reminds me of God's Word

Helps me remember the truth

Helps me understand God's truth

Brings Jesus' words to mind

WEEK 30
Live by the Spirit's Power

"But you will receive power when the Holy Spirit comes on you; and you will be my witnesses in Jerusalem, and in all Judea and Samaria, and to the ends of the earth." - Acts 1:8

BIG TRUTH: The Holy Spirit gives God's people power to live for Jesus and share the good news.

WARM-UP: Have you ever tried to do something good, but you ran out of courage?

Maybe you wanted to:

✝ stand up for someone

✝ tell the truth

✝ apologize first

✝ invite a new kid to play

✝ talk about Jesus

✝ but you felt nervous.

Acts 1:8 teaches that God doesn't leave His people to do hard things alone. God gives help, real help, through the Holy Spirit.

What Acts 1:8 Is Saying

Jesus spoke these words to His followers before He returned to heaven. He told them two key things:

1. **"You will receive power when the Holy Spirit has come on you."**

   This power is not about muscles or being loud. It's God's strength to obey, to love, and to be brave.

2. **"You will be my witnesses."**

   A witness is someone who tells what they know is true.

A witness doesn't need fancy words. A witness simply tells the truth: "This is who Jesus is. This is what He did. This is why it matters."

What Kind of Power Is This?

Some people imagine power as lightning or super strength. But the Spirit's power often looks like everyday courage.

Spirit power can help you:

✟ tell the truth when lying would be easier

✟ forgive instead of getting revenge

✟ say "no" to temptation

✟ pray when you feel anxious

✟ speak kindly when you feel irritated

✟ share your faith without fear

This is not "look at me" power. This is "look at Jesus" power.

What Does It Mean to Be a Witness?

Being a witness for Jesus doesn't mean you have to preach a long speech in front of your class.

It can mean:

✟ telling a friend, "Jesus is important to me"

✟ sharing one Bible verse that helped you

✟ inviting a friend to church or youth group

✟ answering a question honestly

✟ showing love that matches Jesus' ways

You can also be a witness by how you live. People notice kindness, honesty, patience, and courage.

Witnesses Start Where They Are

Acts 1:8 talks about sharing near and far. But the main point is this: you start where you are.

Your "where you are" might be:

- ✟ your home
- ✟ your classroom
- ✟ your team
- ✟ your neighborhood
- ✟ your friend group

God can use kids too. You don't need to be older to be faithful.

What If I Feel Scared?

It's normal to feel nervous. Even Jesus' followers were afraid at times.

The goal is not "never feel fear." The goal is: trust God and take one brave step anyway.

A simple prayer can be: "Holy Spirit, please give me courage and the right words."

Tiny Step to Try This Week

Pick one way to be a witness this week. Keep it small and real:

- ✟ tell someone you're praying for them
- ✟ share one sentence about Jesus
- ✟ do one brave act of kindness
- ✟ Then thank God for His help.

WORKBOOK ACTIVITIES

1) Verse Copy (Handwriting Practice)

Copy the Bible focus phrase:

"But you will receive power when the Holy Spirit comes on you; and you will be my witnesses in Jerusalem, and in all Judea and Samaria, and to the ends of the earth." - **Acts 1:8**

Copy it one more time:

____

____

____

____

2) Fill in the Blanks

"You will receive ____________________________ when the Holy

____________________________ has comes on you, and

you will be my ____________________________."

Word bank: power, Spirit, witnesses

3) Match the Word to the Meaning

Draw lines to match.

1. Power
2. Witness
3. Holy Spirit

A) tells what is true

B) God's help to obey and be brave

C) God's Helper who strengthens His people

4) True or False

Circle **True** or **False**.

1. The Holy Spirit gives God's people power.   **True / False**

2. A witness must use big, fancy words.   **True / False**

3. The Spirit can help me be brave.   **True / False**

4. Only adults can be witnesses for Jesus.   **True / False**

5) **Spirit Power in Real Life (Circle the Best Choice)**

1. You are tempted to lie.

    A) lie

    B) ask God for help and tell the truth

2. Someone is being left out.

    A) ignore it

    B) include them and show kindness

3. You feel nervous to talk about Jesus.

    A) stay silent forever

    B) take one small step and trust God

4. You feel angry.

    A) explode

    B) pause, pray, and use calm words

6) **My Witness Plan (Write It)**

Write one person you can show Jesus' love to this week:

____

Write one simple witness action you will take:

____

____

Write when you will do it (day/time):

____

____

7) **What Can I Say? (Short Practice)**

Finish these sentences in your own words:

    ✝ "Jesus is important to me because _________________________ ."

    ✝ "I believe Jesus ____ ."

    ✝ "One Bible verse that helps me is _______________________ ."

8) Prayer Practice

Write a prayer (6–10 lines):

"Holy Spirit, thank You for giving power to God's people.

____

____

Please help me obey Jesus today.

____

____

Give me courage to be a witness at

____

____

Help me speak with kindness and truth.

____

____

Amen."

9) Knowledge Check (One-Minute Review)

Answer in one short sentence:

What does Acts 1:8 teach you about what the Holy Spirit gives and what Christians do?

____

____

____

The Holy Spirit Helps Me Be a Witness!

Acts 1:8

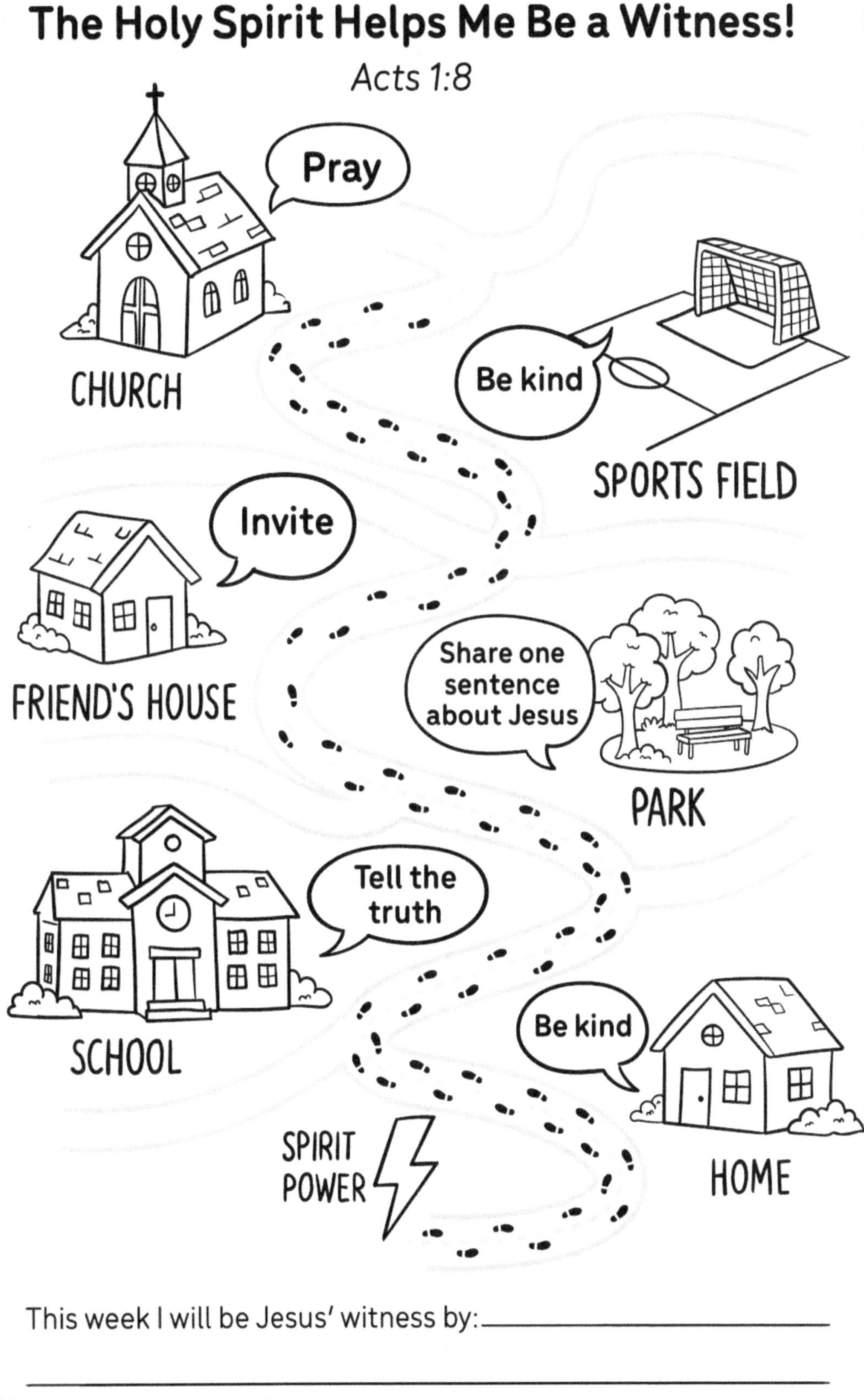

This week I will be Jesus' witness by:_______________________

____

WEEK 31
Grow the Spirit's Fruit

"But the fruit of the Spirit is love, joy, peace, forbearance, kindness, goodness, faithfulness, 23 gentleness and self-control. Against such things there is no law." - Galatians 5:22-23

BIG TRUTH: The Holy Spirit grows Christlike character in God's children, little by little, like fruit growing on a tree.

WARM-UP: Have you ever planted something or watched something grow?

At first, you don't see much. Then one day you notice: "Wait... it's bigger!"

That's how spiritual growth often works too. God grows His children over time. Galatians 5 calls these changes "the fruit of the Spirit."

What Galatians 5:22-23 Is Saying

This passage lists the "fruit of the Spirit," which means the good character God produces in His people:

✝ **Love** - caring for others the way God calls you to

✝ **Joy** - deep gladness that doesn't depend on a perfect day

✝ **Peace** - calm trust in God, even when things feel hard

✝ **Patience** - waiting without snapping

✝ **Kindness** - choosing gentle, helpful actions

✝ **Goodness** - doing what is right

✝ **Faithfulness** - being steady and trustworthy

✝ **Gentleness** - strength under control

✝ **Self-control** - saying "no" to sin and "yes" to what is right

Notice it says **fruit** (singular), but then it lists many parts. It's like one basket of fruit with different kinds inside. God grows all of it in His children.

Fruit Is Not the Same as "Trying Harder"

You do need to make choices, but fruit is not mostly about willpower.

Fruit is what grows when you stay close to God:

- ✟ you read His Word
- ✟ you pray
- ✟ you confess sin and turn back
- ✟ you obey in small steps
- ✟ you keep going even when you mess up

A tree doesn't squeeze itself and shout, "Fruit!" Fruit grows because the tree is alive and being fed.

In the same way, the Spirit grows fruit in you because God has given you new life in Christ.

What If I Don't Feel Like I'm Growing?

Some weeks you'll notice growth. Some weeks you won't.

Ask yourself:

- ✟ Am I spending time with God's Word?
- ✟ Am I praying honestly?
- ✟ Am I admitting sin instead of hiding it?
- ✟ Am I trying one small obedience step at a time?

God is patient with His children. Growth is real, even if it's slow.

A Kid Picture That Helps

Think about brushing your teeth. One time doesn't change much. But doing it every day changes a lot over time.

Growing the Spirit's fruit is like that. Daily small choices add up.

Tiny Step to Try This Week

Pick **one** fruit to practice this week. Don't try to do all nine at once. Pray each day:

"Holy Spirit, please grow ______________________________ in me today."

WORKBOOK ACTIVITIES

1) Verse Copy (Handwriting Practice)

Copy part of the fruit list (or the whole list if you want):

"But the fruit of the Spirit is love, joy, peace, forbearance, kindness, goodness, faithfulness, gentleness and self-control. Against such things there is no law." - **Galatians 5:22-23**

Copy it one more time:

____

____

____

____

2) Fill in the Blank

"The fruit of the______________ is ______________________ ."

Write the missing words: ______________________________

3) True or False

Circle **True** or **False**.

1. The Spirit helps God's children grow.   **True / False**

2. "Fruit" means God changes our character over time.   **True / False**

3. If I mess up once, God stops helping me grow.   **True / False**

4. Gentleness can be strong.   **True / False**

4) Fruit Match (Word to Meaning)

Draw lines to match.

1. Patience   A) doing what is right

2. Kindness   B) waiting without snapping

3. Self-control   C) choosing gentle, helpful actions

4. Goodness   D) controlling your words and choices

5) Spot the Fruit (Circle the Best Choice)

1. Your sibling annoys you.

    A) yell right away

    B) pause and use patience

2. A new kid sits alone.

    A) ignore them

    B) show kindness and include them

3. You want to cheat.

    A) do it

    B) use self-control and be honest

4. A friend is sad.

    A) say "whatever"

    B) show love and care

5. Someone insults you.

    A) insult back

    B) use gentleness and peace

6) My "One Fruit" Plan

Choose **one** fruit to focus on this week (circle one):

Love / Joy / Peace / Patience / Kindness / Goodness
Faithfulness / Gentleness / Self-control

Write one way you can practice it:

- ✞ At home _______________________________________
- ✞ At school _______________________________________
- ✞ With friends ___________________________________

7) **Fruit Check-In (Write It)**

Finish these sentences:

- ✞ Today I saw love when ___________________________

  ____

- ✞ Today I needed self-control when_________________

  ____

- ✞ Tomorrow I want to practice ____________________

  ____

8) **Prayer Practice**

Write a prayer (6–10 lines):

"Holy Spirit, thank You for helping me grow.

____

____

Please grow ____________ in my heart this week.

____

____

Help me make wise choices when I feel tempted.

____

____

Help me become more like Jesus.

____

____

Amen."

9) **Knowledge Check (One-Minute Review)**

Answer in one short sentence:

What is the fruit of the Spirit?

____

____

____

Grow the Fruit of the Spirit!

Galatians 5:22–23

WEEK 32
Hear the Spirit's Guidance

"For those who are led by the Spirit of God are the children of God."
- Romans 8:14

Big Truth: God leads His children by His Spirit, helping them choose what is right and stay close to Jesus.

Warm-Up: Have you ever needed directions?

Maybe you were in a new place and didn't know which way to go. Or you were building something and needed instructions. Good guidance keeps you from getting lost.

Romans 8:14 teaches that God doesn't leave His children to guess their way through life. God leads His people by His Spirit.

What Romans 8:14 Is Saying

This verse says, "For those who are led by the Spirit of God are the children of God."

It's talking about belonging to God's family.

It teaches this truth: **God's children are guided by God's Spirit.**

That doesn't mean God's children always make perfect choices. But it does mean the Spirit is at work:

✝ pointing them toward what is right

✝ warning them away from sin

✝ reminding them of truth

✝ helping them repent when they mess up

What Does It Mean to Be "Led"?

Being led by the Spirit does not mean you get a secret message about which socks to wear.

Most of the time, being led by the Spirit looks like:

- ✟ understanding Scripture
- ✟ choosing obedience
- ✟ feeling convicted about sin
- ✟ growing in the fruit of the Spirit
- ✟ gaining wisdom for decisions

The Spirit guides you toward Jesus, not toward showing off.

How the Spirit Guides You (Three Main Ways)

Here are three clear ways God guides His children:

1. **Through God's Word**

   The Spirit will not guide you to do something the Bible says is wrong.

2. **Through wise counsel**

   God often uses parents, pastors, teachers, and mature Christians to help you.

3. **Through conviction and peace**

   When you're heading toward sin, you may feel an inner warning: "This is wrong."

   When you choose obedience, you often feel peace, even if the choice is hard.

Conviction is not meant to crush you. It's meant to bring you back.

Testing "Guidance"

Sometimes people say, "God told me" when it's really just what they wanted.

A good test is:

- ✟ Does it match Scripture?
- ✟ Does it lead me toward love, truth, and holiness?
- ✟ Does it make me humble, or proud?
- ✟ Would wise Christians agree this is wise?

God's Spirit leads God's children into truth and obedience.

What If I Ignore the Spirit?

Kids can ignore guidance. Adults can too.

When you ignore the Spirit's leading, you often:

- ✟ get into trouble
- ✟ feel more tangled in sin
- ✟ hurt relationships
- ✟ feel spiritually "stuck"

But here's hope: when you confess and repent, God welcomes you back. God's Spirit helps you return.

Tiny Step to Try This Week

Before a tough choice, pause and pray: "Holy Spirit, lead me into what is right." Then choose the wise step that matches God's Word.

WORKBOOK ACTIVITIES

1) Verse Copy (Handwriting Practice)

Copy the Bible focus verse:

"For those who are led by the Spirit of God are the children of God."

Romans 8:14

Copy it one more time:

____

____

____

2) Fill in the Blanks

"For those who are led by the _____________________ of God are the _______________ of God."

Word bank: Spirit, children

3) True or False

Circle **True** or **False**.

1. God leads His children by His Spirit. **True / False**

2. The Spirit will guide me to disobey the Bible. **True / False**

3. The Spirit can convict me when I'm heading toward sin. **True / False**

4. Being led by the Spirit means I never need wisdom from others. **True / False**

4) Match the Guidance

Draw lines to match.

1. God's Word A) helps you learn wise steps

2. Wise counsel B) shows what is true and right

3. Conviction C) warns you when something is wrong

5) Led or Not Led? (Circle One)

1. You want to lie, but you remember God loves truth and you tell the truth. **Led / Not led**

2. You feel jealous and decide to gossip about someone. **Led / Not led**

3. You feel tempted, pray for help, and walk away. **Led / Not led**

4. You ignore wise advice and do what you want. **Led / Not led**

6) Decision Time (Write the Wise Step)

Write one wise step for each situation.

1. You're upset and want to send a mean message.

    Wise step: ____

2. You feel pressure to fit in by doing wrong.

    Wise step: ____

3. You feel guilty after sin.

    Wise step: ____

4. You don't know what to do next.

    Wise step: ____

7) My Guidance Plan

Circle one habit that helps you be led by the Spirit:

       A) read Scripture

       B) pray daily

       C) ask a wise adult for help

       D) confess quickly when I sin

       E) choose kindness when I'm annoyed

Write your choice: ___________________________________

Now write when you'll do it this week:

____

____

____

____

8) Prayer Practice

Write a prayer (6–10 lines):

"Holy Spirit, please lead me.

____

____

Help me love what God loves.

____

____

Help me hate what is wrong.

____

____

Guide my choices at ___________________________

____

____

When I sin, help me repent and return.

____

____

Amen."

9) **Knowledge Check (One-Minute Review)**

Answer in one short sentence:

What does Romans 8:14 teach you about God's children?

____

____

____

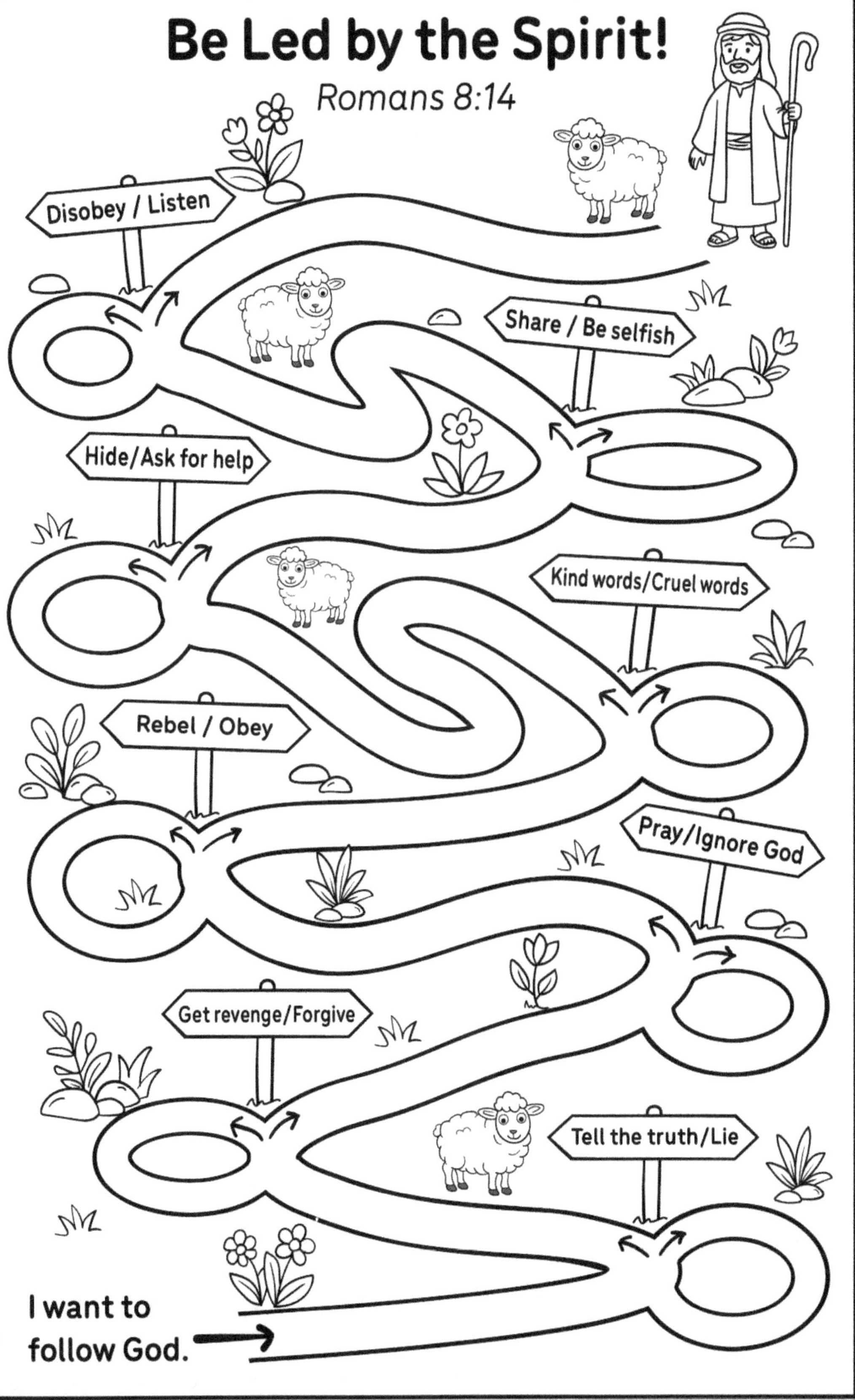

Be Led by the Spirit!
Romans 8:14
Disobey / Listen
Share / Be selfish
Hide/Ask for help
Kind words/Cruel words
Rebel / Obey
Pray/Ignore God
Get revenge/Forgive
Tell the truth/Lie
I want to follow God.

PART SEVEN
The Church and God's People

WEEK 33
Love the Church Family

"And let us consider how we may spur one another on toward love and good deeds, not giving up meeting together, as some are in the habit of doing, but encouraging one another—and all the more as you see the Day approaching." - Hebrews 10:24–25

BIG TRUTH: God made the church to help believers love Jesus, grow in faith, and encourage one another.

WARM-UP: Think about a team you've seen: sports, choir, band, or a school club. A good team isn't just a bunch of people standing near each other. A good team helps each person grow and do their part.

The church is not a building you visit. The church is God's people: believers who gather to worship Jesus and help each other follow Him.

Hebrews 10:24–25 explains why gathering matters.

What Hebrews 10:24–25 Is Saying

This passage gives us two big instructions:

1. **Encourage each other toward love and good deeds.**

   The verse says, "spur one another on." That means wake each other up, cheer each other on, and help each other keep going.

Christians aren't meant to follow Jesus alone.

2. **Not giving up meeting together.**

   "Giving up" means to skip something important again and again, like it doesn't matter.

God knows we need each other. When we gather with the church, we:

✛ hear God's Word taught

✛ worship together

✛ pray together

✛ serve together

✛ make friends who help us follow Jesus

What Makes the Church a Family?

A family isn't perfect. Families can be messy.

The church family includes people who are still growing. Some are young, some are old. Some are strong in faith, some are new. All of us still need Jesus.

But believers are family because we share:

✛ one Savior (Jesus)

✛ one Father (God)

✛ one Spirit (the Holy Spirit)

✛ one hope (God's promises)

EncouragementWhat It Is (And What It Isn't)

Encouragement is helping someone keep going in what is right.

Encouragement is:

✛ "I'm glad you're here."

✛ "I'm praying for you."

✛ "You did the right thing."

✛ "Keep trusting Jesus."

Encouragement is not:

✛ fake compliments

✛ making fun

✛ pushing someone into sin

✛ gossiping

When you encourage someone, you are building them up, not tearing them down.

Why Some People Stop Meeting Together

Sometimes people skip church because:

- ✛ they feel tired
- ✛ they feel embarrassed
- ✛ they got hurt by someone
- ✛ they feel like they don't belong
- ✛ they think it doesn't matter

Hebrews 10 says it *does* matter. Not because God needs a headcount, but because God loves His people and knows we need help.

If you've ever felt like you didn't belong, remember this: church is not only for "perfect" people. It's for people who need Jesus.

How Kids Can Love the Church Family

Kids can be real helpers in church.

You can:

- ✛ greet people kindly
- ✛ listen during worship
- ✛ pray for someone
- ✛ include other kids
- ✛ help clean up
- ✛ write a kind note
- ✛ show respect to leaders and teachers

Small acts of love matter.

Tiny Step to Try This Week

Pick one person at church to encourage this week. It can be a kid, a teacher, or an older person. Say one kind sentence, or write a short note.

WORKBOOK ACTIVITIES

1) Verse Copy (Handwriting Practice)

Copy part of the Bible focus passage:

"And let us consider how we may spur one another on toward love and good deeds," - **Hebrews 10:24**

Copy it one more time:

____

____

____

2) Fill in the Blanks

"Spur one another on toward ___________and good____________."

Word bank:love, deeds

3) True or False

Circle **True** or **False**.

1. The church is only a building.   True / False
2. God wants believers to encourage each other.   True / False
3. Meeting together helps Christians grow.   True / False
4. Kids can't help the church family.   True / False

4) Church Family Match

Draw lines to match.

1. Worship   A) helping others follow Jesus
2. Encourage   B) singing, praying, honoring God
3. Meet together   C) gathering with other believers
4. Serve   D) building others up with words and actions

5) Encouraging Words (Circle the Encouraging Ones)

Circle the sentences that are encouraging:

- ✟ "I'm glad you came today."
- ✟ "You don't matter."
- ✟ "I'll pray for you."
- ✟ "Keep going. God is with you."
- ✟ "Everyone is laughing at you."
- ✟ "Thank you for helping."

6) My Church Family Plan

Write one way you can love the church family this week:

At church I can: _______________________________________

____

Write one person you can encourage: _______________________

Write what you will say or do:_______________________________

____

7) Don't Neglect (Small Habit)

Circle one habit that helps you stay connected to the church:

A) Show up and participate

B) Say hello to someone new

C) Join a kids' class or group

D) Pray for your church

E) Help serve in a small way

Write your choice: _______________________________________

8) Prayer Practice

Write a prayer (6–10 lines):

"God, thank You for the church family.

____

____

Help me love other believers.

____

____

Help me encourage someone this week.

____

____

Help me not neglect meeting together.

____

____

Help our church honor Jesus.

____

____

Amen."

9) Knowledge Check (One-Minute Review)

Answer in one short sentence:

What do Hebrews 10:24–25 teach you to do with other believers?

____

____

____

Church Is a Family!

Hebrews 10:24–25

Cut-Out

| I'm praying for you. | Thanks for serving. | God is with you. | You matter to God. |

Give one to someone at church this week.

WEEK 34
Use Your Gifts to Serve

"Each of you should use whatever gift you have received to serve others, as faithful stewards of God's grace in its various forms." -
1 Peter 4:10

BIG TRUTH: God gives each believer gifts so they can serve others and help the church grow.

WARM-UP: THINK ABout something you're good at.

Maybe you're good at:

- ✝ drawing
- ✝ listening
- ✝ making people laugh
- ✝ helping younger kids
- ✝ building things
- ✝ encouraging people
- ✝ noticing when someone is left out
- ✝ explaining homework

Sometimes kids think, "That's just me." But 1 Peter 4:10 says gifts are not an accident. God gives gifts on purpose.

What 1 Peter 4:10 Is Saying

This verse says, "Each of you should use whatever gift you have received to serve others, as faithful stewards of God's grace in its various forms."

That means every believer has something God can use. Not everyone has the same gifts, but everyone can serve.

Gifts are not mainly for showing off. Gifts are for helping. God's gifts are tools for love.

Also, a steward is someone who takes care of something that belongs to someone else.

Your gifts are not something you own like a toy that's only yours. Your gifts are something God entrusted to you. God wants you to use them wisely.

"Various forms" means God gives different kinds of gifts to different people. That's good. The church needs many kinds of helpers.

Serving Is What Love Looks Like

Serving means doing good for someone else, even when it costs you time or effort.

Serving can look small:

- holding a door
- helping clean up
- sharing supplies
- welcoming someone new
- helping a sibling with a chore
- praying for a friend
- being patient with a younger kid

Small service is still real service.

Gifts Can Be Seen or Quiet

Some gifts are noticeable:

- singing
- playing an instrument
- speaking
- acting in a play

Other gifts are quiet but powerful:

✞ being faithful

✞ showing mercy

✞ encouraging

✞ helping behind the scenes

✞ being a peacemaker

God sees all faithful service, even when other people don't clap.

Serving Is Not About Being the Boss

Some kids think serving means becoming someone's servant like you're "less."

But Christian service is different. Jesus Himself served. Serving is strength used for love.

You can serve without being walked over. You can serve while still being wise. You can serve while still saying "no" to wrong things.

How to Find Ways to Serve

A good way to start is to ask two questions:

1. What needs do I notice?
2. What can I do to help?

Then ask a grown-up or church leader for ideas.

Tiny Step to Try This Week

Choose one gift you have and use it to serve one person this week. Then thank God for the chance to help.

WORKBOOK ACTIVITIES

1) **Verse Copy (Handwriting Practice)**

Copy the Bible focus verse:

"Each of you should use whatever gift you have received to serve others, as faithful stewards of God's grace in its various forms."

1 Peter 4:10

Copy it one more time:

____

____

____

____

2) **Fill in the Blanks**

"Whatever __________ you have received to __________ others."

Word bank: gift, serve

3) **True or False**

Circle **True** or **False**.

1. God gives gifts so we can show off.   **True / False**
2. God gives different gifts to different people.   **True / False**
3. Serving is one way to love others.   **True / False**
4. Only adults can serve in the church.   **True / False**

4) **Match the Word to the Meaning**

Draw lines to match.

1. Gift   A) using time and effort to help others
2. Serve   B) something God gives you to use
3. Steward   C) someone who takes care of what belongs to another

5) Gifts I Notice (Circle Your Strengths)

Circle any that fit you:

✚ encouraging words

✚ helping hands

✚ creativity (art, building, writing)

✚ leadership (helping a group)

✚ listening well

✚ being patient

✚ being brave

✚ making peace

✚ teaching/explaining

✚ noticing who is left out

Now write two you circled:

____

____

6) Serve in Real Life (Write One Idea)

For each place, write one way you can serve.

At home, I can serve by ______________________________

At school, I can serve by ______________________________

At church, I can serve by ______________________________

7) "Good Stewards" Choices (Circle the Best Choice)

1. You're good at art.

    A) refuse to share it

    B) use it to make an encouraging card

2. You're good at noticing people left out.

    A) ignore them

    B) invite them to join

3. You're strong and fast.

    A) brag about it

    B) help someone who is struggling

4. You're good at explaining things.

    A) make others feel dumb

    B) help kindly

8) My One-Service Plan

Write one person you will serve this week:

____

____

Write what you will do:

____

____

Write when you will do it:

____

____

9) Prayer Practice

Write a prayer (6–10 lines):

"God, thank You for giving gifts to Your people.

____

____

Help me be a good steward.

____

____

Show me how to use my gifts to serve others.

____

____

Help me serve with joy and humility.

____

____

Amen."

10) Knowledge Check (One-Minute Review)

Answer in one short sentence:

What does 1 Peter 4:10 teach you to do with your gifts?

____

____

____

God Gave Me Gifts to Serve!

① My Gifts

- ☐ Helping
- ☐ Encouraging
- ☐ Sharing
- ☐ Listening
- ☐ Praying
- ☐ Welcoming
- ☐ Cleaning
- ☐ Drawing
- ☐ Singing
- ☐ Building
- ☐ Teaching
- ☐ Kindness
- ☐ Patience
- ☐ Organizing
- ☐ Making Peace
- ☐ Caring
- ☐ Noticing Needs
- ☐ Working Together

② Needs I Notice

Someone who feels left out	A messy space	A person who needs encouragement

③ My Service Plan

This week I will serve ________________________

by ________________________ on ________________________.

1 Peter 4:10

WEEK 35
Practice Baptism and Communion

"And he took bread, gave thanks and broke it, and gave it to them, saying, "This is my body given for you; do this in remembrance of me.'" - Luke 22:19

BIG TRUTH: Baptism and Communion are special church practices that help Christians remember and show what Jesus has done.

WARM-UP: Have you ever done something to remember an important moment?

People do that with:

✝ photos

✝ trophies

✝ birthday candles

✝ special songs

✝ family traditions

God gave the church two special practices (sometimes called ordinances) that help Christians remember and show the good news: **baptism** and **communion**.

What Luke 22:19 Is Saying

On the night before Jesus died, He ate a meal with His disciples. He took bread, gave thanks, and said, "This is my body, which is given for you. Do this in remembrance of me."

Jesus was teaching them something important:

✝ He was going to give His life.

✝ His people should remember His sacrifice.

Communion is one way Christians obey Jesus' command to remember.

What Is Baptism?

Baptism is when a believer is washed with water in the name of the Father, Son, and Holy Spirit.

Baptism does not save you. Only Jesus saves. Baptism is a sign that shows what God has already done in your heart.

Baptism pictures:

✝ your old life being washed away

✝ your new life in Christ

✝ belonging to Jesus and His people

It's like saying, "I belong to Jesus."

What Is Communion?

Communion is when believers eat bread and drink from the cup (often juice) to remember Jesus' body and blood given for us.

Communion is not a snack time. It's a serious and joyful time of remembering.

Communion helps Christians:

✝ remember the cross

✝ thank Jesus for forgiveness

✝ examine their hearts (confess sin)

✝ rejoice that Jesus is alive

✝ look forward to Jesus' return

Why These Practices Matter

Baptism and Communion help the church keep the gospel clear.

They show that:

- ✝ Jesus really came in the flesh
- ✝ Jesus really died for sinners
- ✝ Jesus really rose again
- ✝ salvation is by faith in Jesus
- ✝ Christians belong to a church family

They also help kids and adults remember that Christianity isn't only ideas. It's real life with Jesus.

Can Kids Participate?

Different churches have different practices.

Some churches baptize believers when they can clearly explain their faith. Some baptize babies as a sign of God's covenant promises. (Families should follow their church's teaching.)

Communion also varies. Many churches invite believers who understand the meaning and can take it respectfully.

The important thing for this book is: talk with your parents and church leaders. Ask questions. God is not bothered by honest questions.

Tiny Step to Try This Week

Ask a parent or trusted adult:

- ✝ "What does baptism mean in our church?"
- ✝ "What does communion mean?"
- ✝ Then write down what you learn.

WORKBOOK ACTIVITIES

1) Verse Copy (Handwriting Practice)

Copy the Bible focus verse:

"Do this in remembrance of me." - **Luke 22:19**

Copy it one more time:

____

____

2) Fill in the Blank

"Do this in _______________________________of me."

Write the missing word:___________________________

3) True or False

Circle **True** or **False**.

1. Baptism saves you from sin. **True / False**

2. Communion helps Christians remember Jesus' sacrifice. **True / False**

3. Baptism is a sign of belonging to Jesus. **True / False**

4. Communion should be treated with respect. **True / False**

4) Baptism or Communion? (Circle One)

1. Uses water as a sign. **Baptism / Communion**

2. Uses bread and cup to remember Jesus. **Baptism / Communion**

3. Shows that someone belongs to Christ and His people. **Baptism / Communion**

4. Obeys Jesus' command: "Do this in remembrance of me." **Baptism / Communion**

5) What Do They Point To? (Match It)

Draw lines to match.

1. Baptism   A) Jesus' death for sinners

2. Communion   B) new life in Christ and belonging

3. Bread   C) remembering Jesus' body given

4. Cup   D) remembering Jesus' blood shed

6) Respect Check (Circle the Best Choice)

1. During communion, the right attitude is:

    A) silly and loud

    B) thankful and focused

2. If you have questions about baptism or communion:

    A) keep quiet forever

    B) ask your parents or church leaders

3. If you sinned and feel guilty:

    A) hide from God

    B) confess to God and trust Jesus' forgiveness

7) My Questions (Write Two)

Write two questions you want to ask about baptism or communion:

____

____

Write who you will ask:____

8) Remembrance Reflection

Write three short phrases you want to remember about Jesus:

1. Jesus____ .

2. Jesus____ .

3. Jesus____ .

9) Prayer Practice

Write a prayer (6–10 lines):

"Jesus, thank You for giving Your body and blood for sinners.

____

____

Thank You for the cross and the resurrection.

____

____

Help me remember You with gratitude.

____

____

Help me honor You when the church practices baptism and communion.

____

____

Amen."

10) Knowledge Check (One-Minute Review)

Answer in one short sentence:

Why did Jesus tell His disciples to remember Him?

____

____

____

Do This in Remembrance of Me

One thing I thank Jesus for: _______________________

____

One sin I can confess to God: _____________________

____

One way I want to live this week: __________________

____

Talk together about your church's practice of baptism and communion.

Luke 22:19

WEEK 36
Share the Good News

"He said to them, "Go into all the world and preach the gospel to all creation." - Mark 16:15

BIG TRUTH: Jesus calls His followers to share the gospel, the good news, so others can know Him too.

WARM-UP: Have you ever found something so good you couldn't keep it to yourself?

Maybe it was:

- ✟ a new game
- ✟ a great book
- ✟ a funny video
- ✟ a restaurant you loved
- ✟ a cool place to visit

Good news spreads because people want others to enjoy it too.

Mark 16:15 tells us Christians have the best news of all to share: the gospel.

What "Gospel" Means

"Gospel" means **good news**.

The gospel is the good news that:

- ✟ God made us
- ✟ we sinned and need rescue
- ✟ Jesus came as Savior and King
- ✟ Jesus died for sinners
- ✟ Jesus rose again
- ✟ everyone who repents and trusts Jesus can be forgiven and have new life

That is not a small message. That is life-changing news.

What Mark 16:15 Is Saying

Jesus tells His followers: "Go... and preach the gospel."

It doesn't mean you have to be loud and pushy. It means you tell the truth clearly.

And Jesus says "all the world," which means the gospel is for every kind of person. God wants people from every nation and background to hear about Jesus.

How Kids Can Share the Good News

Kids sometimes think evangelism is only for missionaries or pastors. But kids can share too.

Here are some kid-sized ways:

- ✝ tell a friend you go to church and why
- ✝ share a Bible verse that helped you
- ✝ invite a friend to church or a kids' event
- ✝ ask a friend if you can pray for them
- ✝ explain Easter or Christmas in one sentence
- ✝ show kindness that makes people curious about Jesus

You don't need to know everything. You only need to tell what you know is true.

A Simple Gospel Sentence You Can Use

Try this one: "Jesus is God's Son. He died for sinners and rose again, and He forgives everyone who trusts Him."

That's clear and simple.

Sharing the Gospel Takes Courage

Sometimes you might feel:

- ✝ embarrassed
- ✝ nervous
- ✝ worried about being laughed at
- ✝ unsure what to say

That's normal. Remember Acts 1:8: the Holy Spirit helps Jesus' witnesses.

You can pray:

"God, give me courage and kindness."

What If Someone Says No?

Not everyone will listen. Some people will say they don't care. Some may be rude.

Your job is not to force them. Your job is to be faithful and loving.

- ✝ be respectful
- ✝ tell the truth
- ✝ answer kindly
- ✝ pray for them
- ✝ keep loving them

God is the One who changes hearts.

Tiny Step to Try This Week

Choose one person to pray for by name. Ask God for a chance to share one true sentence about Jesus or to invite them to church.

WORKBOOK ACTIVITIES

1) Verse Copy (Handwriting Practice)

Copy the Bible focus verse:

"He said to them, "Go into all the world and preach the gospel to all creation."- **Mark 16:15**

Copy it one more time:

____

____

____

____

2) Fill in the Blanks

"Preach the _________________________ to all _______________."

Word bank:gospel, creation

3) True or False

Circle **True** or **False**.

1. The gospel means good news.   **True / False**
2. Only adults can share the gospel.   **True / False**
3. We should be kind and respectful when sharing
   Jesus.   **True / False**
4. My job is to force people to believe.   **True / False**

4) Gospel Basics (Match It)

Draw lines to match.

1. God   A) rose again
2. Sin   B) made us
3. Jesus   C) separates us from God
4. Resurrection   D) died for sinners

5) Build Your Gospel Sentence (Fill In)

Fill in the blanks:

"Jesus is God's _________________. He _______________ for sinners and _____________________ again. He forgives everyone who _____________________ Him."

Word bank: Son, died, rose, trusts

6) Who Can I Share With?

Write 3 people you can pray for:

1. ____
2. ____
3. ____

Circle one person you will pray for every day this week.

7) **What Could I Say? (Choose One and Write It)**

Choose one option and write it in your own words.

    A) Invite "Do you want to come to church with me?"

    B) Share "Jesus is important to me because _______________ ."

    C) Offer prayer "Can I pray for you about _______________ ?"

My sentence: _______________________________________

____

____

____

____

8) **Courage Practice**

Circle the best response:

If I feel nervous about sharing Jesus, I can:

    A) give up forever

    B) pray and take one small step

    C) be rude and loud

Write one short prayer for courage:

God, please help me

____

____

9) **Prayer Practice**

Write a prayer (6–10 lines):

"God, thank You for the gospel.

____

____

Thank You that Jesus died and rose again.

____

____

Please help me share the good news with kindness.

____

____

Give me courage to speak when I have a chance.

____

____

Help _____________________ Jesus.

Amen."

10) Knowledge Check (One-Minute Review)

Answer in one short sentence:

What does Mark 16:15 teach Jesus' followers to do?

____

____

____

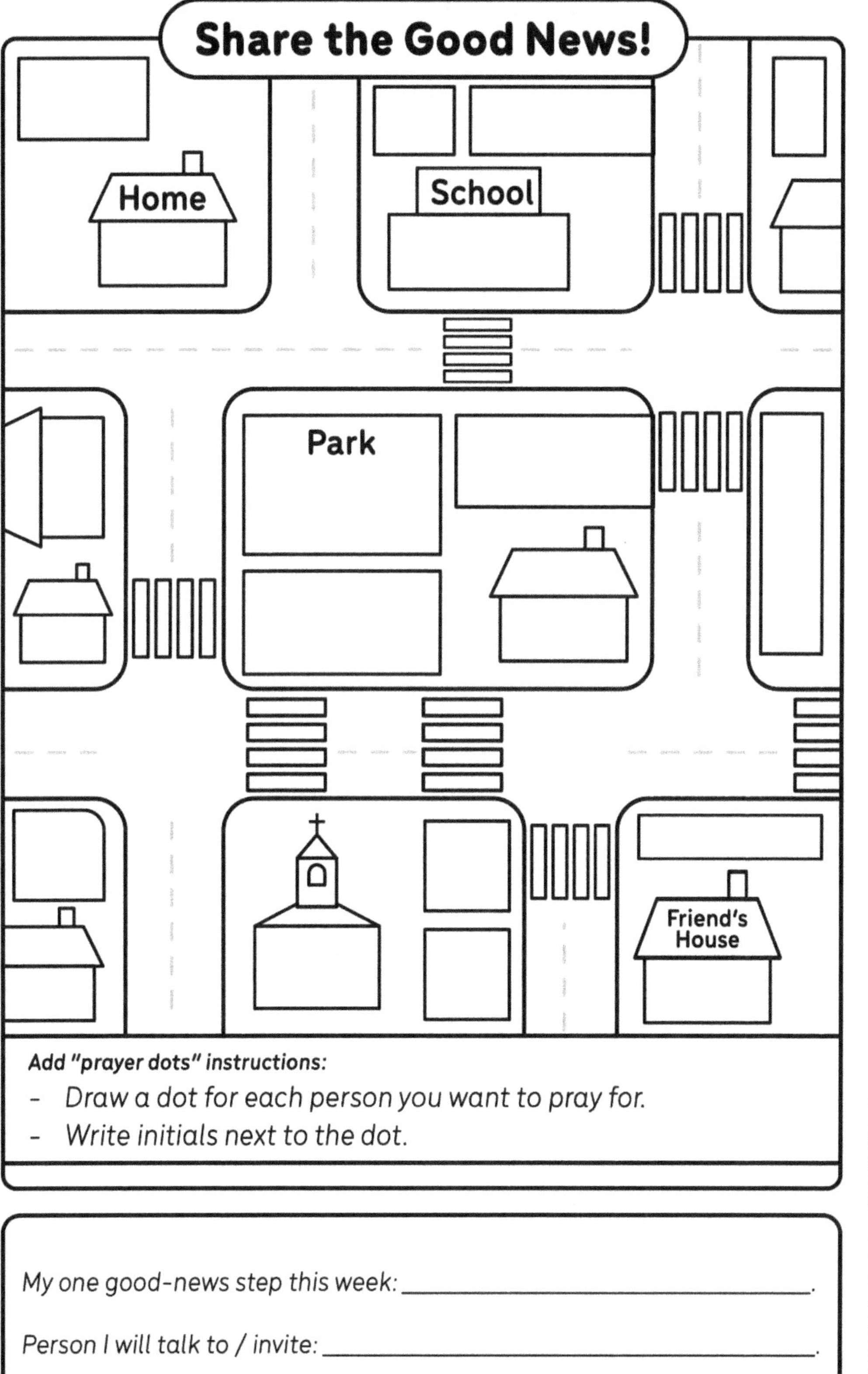

Share the Good News!
Home
School
Park
Friend's House
Add "prayer dots" instructions:
- Draw a dot for each person you want to pray for.
- Write initials next to the dot.
My one good-news step this week: ______________________.
Person I will talk to / invite: ______________________.
Mark 16:15

WEEK 37
Make Peace and Forgive

"Be kind and compassionate to one another, forgiving each other, just as in Christ God forgave you." - Ephesians 4:32

BIG TRUTH: Because God forgave us in Christ, we can forgive others and work toward peace.

WARM-UP: Have you ever had a friendship feel awkward after someone hurt you?

Maybe someone:

- ✝ said something mean
- ✝ left you out
- ✝ blamed you
- ✝ broke your trust
- ✝ embarrassed you

When that happens, it's easy to think, "I'm done with them."

Ephesians 4:32 gives a different path: kindness, tender hearts, forgiveness, and peace.

What Ephesians 4:32 Is Saying

This verse gives three clear commands:

1. **Be kind to one another**

   Kindness is choosing helpful, gentle actions and words.

2. **Be compassionate**

   This means your heart is not hard like a rock. You care. You don't enjoy someone else's pain.

3. **Forgive one another**

> Forgiveness means you choose not to hold someone's sin over their head forever.

Then it gives the reason:just as in Christ God forgave you.

This is the biggest part. God forgave you through Jesus. God didn't forgive because you were perfect. He forgave because Jesus took your sin.

So Christians forgive because they have been forgiven.

What Forgiveness Is (And What It Isn't)

Forgiveness can be confusing, so let's make it clear.

Forgiveness is:

- ✟ letting go of revenge
- ✟ choosing not to keep punishing someone in your heart
- ✟ being willing to move toward peace when possible
- ✟ trusting God with justice

Forgiveness is not:

- ✟ pretending it didn't happen
- ✟ saying the sin was okay
- ✟ instantly trusting someone who is still hurting you
- ✟ staying in an unsafe situation

If someone is hurting you badly or repeatedly, you should tell a trusted adult. Forgiveness does not mean you hide harm.

What Does "Make Peace" Mean?

Peace is not just "no yelling." Peace is relationships being set right.

Making peace can include:

- ✟ admitting what you did wrong
- ✟ apologizing without excuses
- ✟ listening to the other person

✝ forgiving

✝ choosing kind words afterward

✝ asking a wise adult for help if needed

Sometimes peace is quick. Sometimes it takes time. But God calls His people to seek peace, not to feed drama.

A Kid Picture That Helps

Think of a knot in a rope. A knot makes the rope hard to use. Forgiveness is like gently working the knot loose.

It can take patience. But it makes the relationship able to move again.

How to Forgive (A Simple Plan)

Here are four steps that help:

1. **Tell God the truth.** "God, this hurt me."

2. **Remember the gospel.** "God forgave me in Christ."

3. **Choose forgiveness.** "I will not get revenge."

4. **Take one peace step.** Apologize, talk calmly, or ask for help.

Tiny Step to Try This Week

Think of one relationship that needs peace. Pray one sentence each day: "God, help me forgive and make peace like You forgave me."

WORKBOOK ACTIVITIES

1) Verse Copy (Handwriting Practice)

Copy the Bible focus verse:

"Be kind and compassionate to one another, forgiving each other, just as in Christ God forgave you." - **Ephesians 4:32**

Copy it one more time:

____

____

____

____

2) Fill in the Blanks

"Be _______________ and _______________ to one another,

_______________ each other, just as in Christ God _______________ you."

Word bank:kind, compassionate, forgiving, forgave

3) True or False

Circle **True** or **False**.

1. Forgiveness means pretending sin is okay.   **True / False**

2. God forgives Christians in Christ.   **True / False**

3. Forgiveness means I must trust someone instantly. **True / False**

4. Kindness and tenderheartedness help make peace. **True / False**

4) Match the Word to the Meaning

Draw lines to match.

1. Kind   A) letting go of revenge

2. Tenderhearted   B) gentle and caring

3. Forgive   C) choosing helpful words and actions

5) Forgive or Not? (Circle the Better Choice)

1. Someone bumps you by accident.

    A) yell
    B) forgive and move on

2. A friend says something unkind and then apologizes.

   A) hold it over them forever

   B) forgive and work toward peace

3. Someone keeps hurting you and you feel unsafe.

   A) keep quiet

   B) tell a trusted adult and get help

6) Peace Steps (Write One Step)

Write one peace step you can take in each situation.

1. You were mean to your sibling.

   Peace step: ____

2. A friend left you out.

   Peace step: ____

3. You argued with a parent.

   Peace step: ____

4. You hurt someone online.

   Peace step: ____

7) Apology Practice (Write It)

Write a real apology (no excuses). Use this template:

"I'm sorry for____

____

That was wrong.

____

____

Will you forgive me?

____

____

I will try to _______________________________________ ."

Write a prayer (6–10 lines):

"God, thank You for forgiving me in Christ.

____

____

Please help me forgive _______________________ .

____

Help me let go of revenge.

____

____

Help me take one step toward peace.

____

____

Give me a tender heart.

____

____

Amen."

9) **Knowledge Check (One-Minute Review)**

Answer in one short sentence:

Why does Ephesians 4:32 say Christians should forgive?

____

____

Forgive Like Jesus Forgave You!
Ephesians 4:32
HURT
Tell the truth
Say sorry
Forgive
Pray
Use kind words
PEACE
My One Peace Step
This week I will make peace by

PART EIGHT
Living the Christian Life

WEEK 38
Pray with Confidence

"Do not be anxious about anything, but in every situation, by prayer and petition, with thanksgiving, present your requests to God." -
Philippians 4:6

BIG TRUTH: You can bring every worry and every need to God in prayer, because God listens and cares.

WARM-UP: Have you ever had your mind feel busy, like it won't turn off?

You might worry about:

- ✝ a test
- ✝ a friend problem
- ✝ something happening at home
- ✝ being left out
- ✝ messing up
- ✝ the future

Worry can feel like carrying a heavy backpack you can't take off.

Philippians 4:6 shows a better way:bring your worries to God.

What Philippians 4:6 Is Saying

This verse begins:"Do not be anxious about anything..."

That does not mean "never feel nervous." It means you don't have to live controlled by worry.

Then it says:"but in everything... let your requests be made known to God."

"In everything" means:

- ✞ big things
- ✞ small things
- ✞ school things
- ✞ friend things
- ✞ family things
- ✞ secret fears you don't like to say out loud

God is not bothered when you come to Him. God invites you.

The verse also uses two words:

- ✞ **prayer**
- ✞ **supplication**

Both mean talking to God, asking Him for help. "Supplication" is a big word that means making a request, like saying, "God, please help."

Then it adds:**"with thanksgiving."**

That means prayer isn't only asking. It's also thanking God for who He is and what He has done.

Why You Can Pray with Confidence

Confidence doesn't mean arrogance. It means you are not scared to come to God, because you know God is good.

If you belong to Jesus, you can pray confidently because:

- ✞ God is your Father
- ✞ Jesus opened the way to God
- ✞ the Holy Spirit helps you pray
- ✞ God loves His children
- ✞ God's wisdom is perfect

God may not answer exactly how you expect, but God always listens and always does what is right.

What If I Don't Know What to Say?

That happens to everyone.

Prayer doesn't need fancy words. God is not grading you.

You can pray simple prayers like:

- ✝ "God, help me."
- ✝ "God, I'm scared."
- ✝ "God, please forgive me."
- ✝ "God, thank You."

A helpful prayer shape is:

Praise, Ask, Thanks

- ✝ Praise "God, You are good."
- ✝ Ask "Please help me with _______________________ ."
- ✝ Thanks "Thank You for _______________________ ."

Prayer Changes You

Prayer doesn't only change situations. Prayer also changes you.

When you pray:

- ✝ you remember God is in charge
- ✝ you bring fear into the light
- ✝ you receive peace from God
- ✝ you stop pretending you can control everything

Prayer is not a last resort. Prayer is the first step of faith.

Tiny Step to Try This Week

Set a "prayer moment" once a day (morning, lunchtime, or bedtime). Pray one request and one thank-you every day for seven days.

WORKBOOK ACTIVITIES

1) **Verse Copy (Handwriting Practice)**

Copy the Bible focus verse:

"Do not be anxious about anything, but in every situation, by prayer and petition, with thanksgiving, present your requests to God."

Philippians 4:6

Copy it one more time:

____

____

____

____

2) **Fill in the Blanks**

"Do not be _____________________________ about anything, but in

_____________________________ by prayer..."

Word bank: anxious, every situation

3) **True or False**

Circle **True** or **False**.

1. God only wants to hear about big problems.   **True / False**

2. God invites us to bring requests to Him.   **True / False**

3. Thanksgiving is part of prayer.   **True / False**

4. Prayer must use long, fancy words.   **True / False**

4) **Prayer Words (Match It)**

Draw lines to match.

1. Prayer   A) thanking God

2. Supplication   B) talking to God

3. Thanksgiving   C) asking God for help

5) Worry to Prayer (Write It)

Write one worry you have right now:

____

____

Now turn it into a prayer request:

God, please help me with

____

____

Now add thanksgiving:

Thank You, God, for

____

____

6) What Should I Do? (Circle the Best Choice)

1. I feel anxious about tomorrow.

    A) worry all night
    B) pray and ask God for help

2. I feel guilty after sin.

    A) hide from God
    B) confess and ask forgiveness

3. A friend is struggling.

    A) ignore it
    B) pray and offer help

7) My Daily Prayer Plan

Circle one time you will pray each day this week:

    A) morning
    B) lunchtime
    C) bedtime

Write your plan:

"I will pray each day at ______________________________

______________________________."

8) Prayer Practice (Praise–Ask–Thanks)

Write a short prayer using the three parts (6–10 lines):

Praise:God, You are

____

____

Ask:Please help me with

____

____

Thanks:Thank You for

____

____

____

____

Amen.

9) Knowledge Check (One-Minute Review)

Answer in one short sentence:

What does Philippians 4:6 tell you to do instead of being anxious?

____

____

____

Pray with Confidence!
Philippians 4:6
Worries I Carry
Prayers I Give to God
Worry

WEEK 39
Learn to Thank God Daily

"Give thanks in all circumstances; for this is God's will for you in Christ Jesus." - 1 Thessalonians 5:18

BIG TRUTH: Gratitude is a habit God wants for His children, and it helps your heart stay steady.

WARM-UP: Have you ever noticed how complaining spreads fast?

One person grumbles, then another person joins in, and soon everything feels gloomy, even if some things are good.

Gratitude can spread too. When you learn to thank God, it changes how you see your day.

That's why 1 Thessalonians 5:18 matters.

What 1 Thessalonians 5:18 Is Saying

The verse says, "Give thanks..."

That's a command, not just a suggestion. God wants His people to be thankful.

Then it says, "in all circumstances."

That does **not** mean you have to be happy about bad things. It doesn't mean you pretend pain is fun. It means no matter what is happening, you can still find reasons to thank God, because God is still God.

Then it says, "for this is God's will for you in Christ Jesus."

God wants you to grow into a thankful person. And because you belong to Jesus, gratitude fits your new life.

Thankfulness Isn't the Same as Pretending

Some kids think thankfulness means saying, "Everything is great!" even when it's not.

Real gratitude sounds like:

✞ "This is hard, but God is still with me."

✞ "I'm sad, but God is still good."

✞ "I don't like this situation, but I can thank God for help, people, and hope."

That's honest gratitude.

Why Gratitude Helps Your Heart

Thankfulness does at least three good things:

1. **It reminds you who God is.**

   God is Provider, Helper, Father, Savior.

2. **It fights selfishness.**

   Gratitude says, "I'm not the center. God is good to me."

3. **It helps you notice gifts.**

   When you thank God daily, you start seeing blessings you used to ignore.

What Can You Thank God For?

You can thank God for big things:

✞ salvation in Jesus

✞ forgiveness

✞ church family

✞ God's Word

You can also thank God for everyday things:

✞ food

✞ clean water

✝ friends

✝ a warm bed

✝ a teacher who helps

✝ sunlight

✝ a funny moment

✝ a safe ride home

Gratitude doesn't require a perfect life. It requires open eyes.

A Kid Picture That Helps

Think of your heart like a garden.

Complaining is like planting weeds. Weeds grow fast and take over.

Thankfulness is like planting good seeds. Good seeds grow strong over time.

What you plant most often becomes what grows.

Tiny Step to Try This Week

Start a "three thanks" habit:

Every day, thank God for **three specific things**. Try to pick new ones each day.

WORKBOOK ACTIVITIES

1) Verse Copy (Handwriting Practice)

Copy the Bible focus verse:

"Give thanks in all circumstances; for this is God's will for you in Christ Jesus." - **1 Thessalonians 5:18**

Copy it one more time:

____

____

____

2) Fill in the Blanks

"Give _________________________ in all ____."

Write the missing words: ____

3) True or False

Circle **True** or **False**.

1. God wants His children to be thankful.   **True / False**

2. Thankfulness means pretending hard things are fun.**True / False**

3. You can thank God even on a tough day.   **True / False**

4. Gratitude can help your attitude.   **True / False**

4) Thankful or Complaining? (Circle One)

1. "I never get what I want."   **Thankful / Complaining**

2. "God, thank You for helping me today." **Thankful / Complaining**

3. "This is hard, but I can still trust God." **Thankful / Complaining**

4. "Nothing good ever happens."   **Thankful / Complaining**

5) Three Thanks Today

Write three things you can thank God for today:

1. ____

2. ____

3. ____

Now circle one and write why it matters to you:

____

____

6) All Circumstances (What Can I Thank God For?)

Write one "hard circumstance" and one "thank you" you can still pray.

Hard circumstance:

____

____

Thank You, God, for:

____

____

(Example: "people who help me," "Your presence," "a new day," "Your Word.")

7) Gratitude Plan (Daily Habit)

Circle one plan you will try this week:

      A) Thank God for 3 things at bedtime

      B) Write 3 thanks each morning

      C) Say 3 thanks at dinner

      D) Make a "thank you" list on Sunday

Write your plan:

____

____

8) Prayer Practice

Write a prayer (6–10 lines):

"God, thank You for Your goodness.

____

____

Help me notice Your gifts each day.

____

____

Help me stop complaining and grow gratitude.

Today I thank You for

Amen."

9) Knowledge Check (One-Minute Review)

Answer in one short sentence:

What does 1 Thessalonians 5:18 teach you to do each day?

My Thank-You Wall

WEEK 40
Fight Temptation with God's Word

"Your word is a lamp for my feet, a light on my path." -
Psalm 119:105

BIG TRUTH: God's Word guides you when you're tempted, helping you see the right next step.

WARM-UP: Have you ever walked in a dark room and bumped into something?

In the dark, it's hard to know where to step. You might trip, crash, or get hurt.

Temptation can feel like darkness too. When you're tempted, the wrong choice can look "fine," and the right choice can feel hard to see.

Psalm 119:105 says God's Word is like a lamp and a light. It helps you see what to do next.

What Psalm 119:105 Is Saying

The verse says, "Your word is a lamp for my feet..."

A lamp for your feet helps you see the ground right in front of you. It shows the next safe step.

Then it says, "a light on my path."

A light on your path helps you see where you're going. It helps you avoid danger ahead.

God's Word does both:

✝ it helps with the next choice

✝ it helps with the direction of your life

Why Temptation Feels Strong

Temptation often shows up when:

- ✝ you're tired
- ✝ you're hungry
- ✝ you're angry
- ✝ you feel lonely
- ✝ you want to fit in
- ✝ you want control

In those moments, you might think:

- ✝ "No one will know."
- ✝ "It's not that bad."
- ✝ "I deserve this."
- ✝ "I'll stop later."

Those thoughts are like shadows. God's Word brings light.

Jesus Used God's Word Against Temptation

When Jesus was tempted (you can read about it in the Gospels), He answered with Scripture. He didn't argue with the devil using feelings. He used truth.

That teaches us something important: **God's Word is a strong weapon against lies.**

How to Use God's Word in a Temptation Moment

Here's a simple plan:

1. **Spot the temptation.**

   Name it: "I'm tempted to lie," or "I'm tempted to be mean," or "I'm tempted to gossip."

2. **Shine the light of Scripture.**

   Ask: "What does God's Word say about this?"

   Examples:

- o Tempted to lie? God loves truth.
- o Tempted to be cruel? God calls you to kindness.
- o Tempted to get revenge? God calls you to forgive.
- o Tempted to worry? God calls you to pray.

3. **Take the next right step.**

Walk away. Tell the truth. Ask for help. Pray. Choose kindness.

You may still feel the pull, but you can obey with God's help.

You Won't Remember the Light if You Never Turn It On

A lamp only helps if it's on.

That's why reading and memorizing Scripture matters. When God's Word is in your heart, it's ready when temptation comes.

Even one verse can help you step away from sin.

Tiny Step to Try This Week

Pick one verse that helps you fight temptation. Write it on a card and read it every day. When temptation shows up, say the verse out loud (or quietly) and take one right step.

WORKBOOK ACTIVITIES

1) Verse Copy (Handwriting Practice)

Copy the Bible focus verse:

"Your word is a lamp for my feet, a light on my path."

Psalm 119:105

Copy it one more time:

____

____

2) Fill in the Blanks

"Your word is a ________________ for my ____________________ ,

a ________________ on my ____________________________."

Word bank: lamp, feet, light, path

3) True or False

Circle **True** or **False**.

1. God's Word can guide my choices. **True / False**

2. Temptation always tells the truth. **True / False**

3. A lamp helps you see the next step. **True / False**

4. Memorizing Scripture can help me fight temptation. **True / False**

4) Lamp or Darkness? (Circle One)

1. "No one will know, so it's fine." **Lamp / Darkness**

2. "God loves truth, so I will tell the truth." **Lamp / Darkness**

3. "I'll get revenge because they deserve it." **Lamp / Darkness**

4. "I will forgive as God forgave me." **Lamp / Darkness**

5) Temptation Spotting

Circle two temptations you face most often:

- ✟ lying
- ✟ anger
- ✟ jealousy
- ✟ disrespect
- ✟ gossip
- ✟ laziness
- ✟ mean jokes
- ✟ cheating

Now write one sentence:

"When I am tempted to ________________, God's Word can help me

____________________________________."

6) Choose the Next Step (Circle the Best Choice)

1. You want to lie about homework.

    A) lie

    B) tell the truth and ask for help

2. You want to tease someone to fit in.

    A) tease them

    B) use kind words or walk away

3. You want to scroll something you know is wrong.

    A) keep going

    B) stop and choose what is right

4. You want to explode in anger.

    A) yell

    B) pause, pray, and speak calmly

7) My "Light Verse"

Write one verse (or part of a verse) you want to remember this week:

____

____

____

Write where it is found (example:Psalm 119:105):

____

____

____

8) Prayer Practice

Write a prayer (6–10 lines):

"God, thank You for Your Word.

____

____

Please make it a lamp to my feet and a light to my path.

____

____

Help me spot temptation and choose what is right.

____

____

When I'm tempted to _______________, help me obey You.

____

____

Amen."

9) Knowledge Check (One-Minute Review)

Answer in one short sentence:

What does Psalm 119:105 teach you about God's Word?

____

____

____

God's Word Lights My Way!

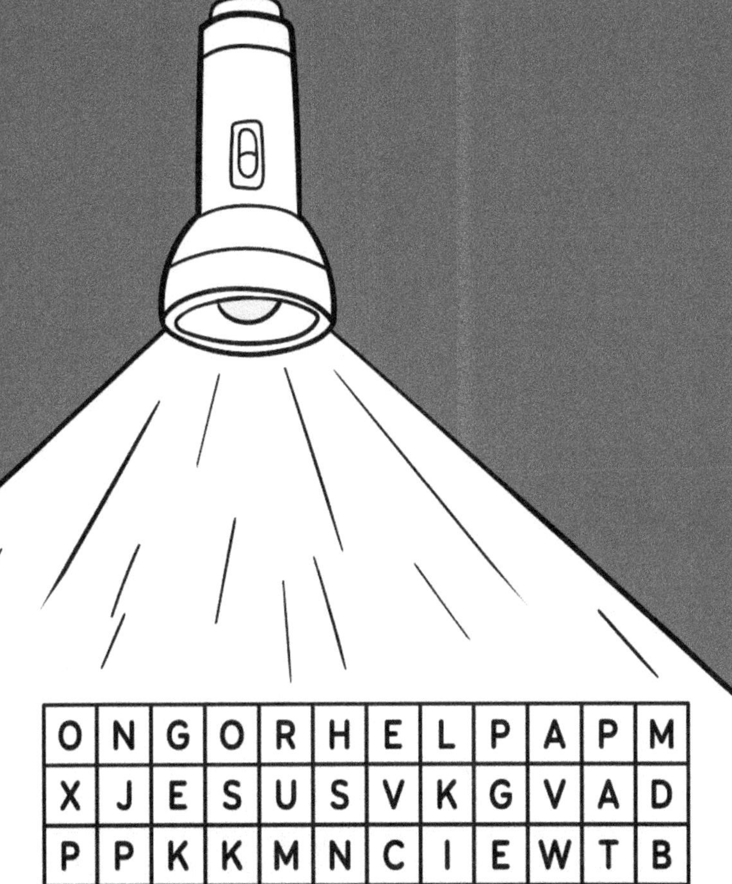

Find the Hidden Words

WORD   PRAY
LAMP   STOP
FEET   KIND
LIGHT   FORGIVE
PATH   OBEY
TRUTH   HELP
WISE   JESUS

One temptation I want God's Word to help me with:

____

My next right step will be:

____

Psalm 119:105

WEEK 41
Practice Self-Control

"Like a city whose walls are broken through is a person who lacks self-control." - Proverbs 25:28

BIG TRUTH: Self-control is strength with a guard on it. God helps you control your words, actions, and choices.

WARM-UP: Have you ever said something and wished you could grab the words and pull them back?

Or done something fast without thinking, then thought, "That was a bad idea"?

That's where self-control matters.

Proverbs 25:28 gives a picture that helps you remember what self-control does.

What Proverbs 25:28 Is Saying

It says a person without self-control is like "a city broken into and left without walls."

In Bible times, a city had walls for protection. Walls kept out enemies and danger.

If a city had no walls, it was easy to attack. Anyone could come in and cause harm.

That's what life is like without self-control:

- ✝ anger runs in and destroys
- ✝ lies slip out
- ✝ temptation pushes you around
- ✝ bad habits take over
- ✝ friends can pressure you easily

Self-control is like rebuilding the walls. It protects your heart and your life.

What Self-Control Is (Kid Words)

Self-control means you can say "no" to what is wrong and "yes" to what is right.

It's not just controlling your body. It includes:

- ✝ your words
- ✝ your attitude
- ✝ your choices
- ✝ what you watch
- ✝ what you repeat
- ✝ how you react

Self-control doesn't mean you never feel strong emotions. It means emotions don't boss you around.

Why Self-Control Can Be Hard

Self-control is hard because:

- ✝ sin pulls at your heart
- ✝ habits feel comfortable
- ✝ you want things fast
- ✝ you want to fit in
- ✝ you want to "win" an argument

But God doesn't leave you alone. The Holy Spirit helps God's children grow fruit, and self-control is one of the Spirit's fruit.

How Self-Control Grows

Self-control grows through practice.

Here are three strong helpers:

1. **Pause**

   Stop for two seconds before you react. That tiny pause can save you from a big mess.

2. **Pray**

   "God, help me." Short prayers count.

3. **Choose the next right step**

   Walk away. Take a breath. Ask for help. Use calm words. Tell the truth.

Small steps build strong walls over time.

Self-Control Isn't Only for "Bad Kids"

Every person needs self-control. Even adults.

Self-control helps you:

- finish work instead of quitting
- do chores without complaining
- speak kindly when annoyed
- avoid sinful media
- handle disappointment
- honor God when nobody is watching

Tiny Step to Try This Week

Pick one area you want God to strengthen:

- anger
- words
- screen choices
- impatience
- lying
- Then practice the "Pause–Pray–Choose" plan every day.

WORKBOOK ACTIVITIES

1) Verse Copy (Handwriting Practice)

Copy the Bible focus verse:

"Like a city whose walls are broken through is a person who lacks self-control."- **Proverbs 25:28**

Copy it one more time:

____

____

____

____

2) Fill in the Blank

"Like a city whose walls are broken through is a person who ______."

Write the missing word: _______________________________________

3) True or False

Circle **True** or **False**.

1. Self-control helps protect my life like a wall
   protects a city. **True / False**

2. Self-control means I never feel angry. **True / False**

3. The Holy Spirit can help me grow self-control. **True / False**

4. A pause before reacting can help me choose wisely. **True / False**

4) Match the Word to the Meaning

Draw lines to match.

1. Self-control   A) protection from harm

2. Walls   B) a small stop before reacting

3. Pause   C) choosing what is right instead of
   reacting

5) Walls or No Walls? (Circle One)

1. You're annoyed and you stop, breathe, then speak calmly.

Walls / No walls

2. You get angry and explode right away.

Walls / No walls

3. You're tempted to cheat and you choose honesty.

Walls / No walls

4. You scroll something you know is wrong and keep going.

Walls / No walls

6) My Self-Control Target

Circle one area you want to grow:

Anger / Words / Screens / Patience / Honesty / Jealousy / Laziness

Write one situation where you need self-control:

____

____

Write one "wall-building" step you will take:

____

____

7) Pause-Pray-Choose Plan

Fill in the blanks:

PAUSE: When I feel tempted, I will

____

____

PRAY: "God, please help me

____

____

CHOOSE: My next right step is

____

____

8) Scenario Practice (Circle the Best Response)

1. Someone insults you.

    A) insult back

    B) pause and use calm words

2. You want to complain about chores.

    A) complain loudly

    B) do it with a better attitude

3. You want to lie about a mistake.

    A) lie

    B) tell the truth and ask forgiveness

4. You feel like quitting homework.

    A) quit

    B) ask for help and keep going

9) Prayer Practice

Write a prayer (6–10 lines):

"God, please help me grow self-control.

____

____

Help me build strong 'walls' in my heart.

____

____

When I feel tempted to ___________, help me pause, pray, and choose what is right.

____

____

Thank You for helping me grow.

____

____

Amen."

10) Knowledge Check (One-Minute Review)

Answer in one short sentence:

What does Proverbs 25:28 teach you about self-control?

____

____

____

Build Strong Walls with Self-Control!

Proverbs 25:28

WEEK 42
Love Your Neighbor

"He answered, "'Love the Lord your God with all your heart and with all your soul and with all your strength and with all your mind'; and, 'Love your neighbor as yourself.'" - Luke 10:27

BIG TRUTH: Loving your neighbor means choosing real care and kindness for the people God puts near you.

WARM-UP: When you hear the word "neighbor," you might think of the people who live next door.

But in the Bible, "neighbor" often means something bigger:the people around you—at school, at home, on your street, in your church, on your team.

Luke 10:27 tells us that love for God and love for neighbor belong together.

What Luke 10:27 Is Saying

This verse gives two commands:

1. **Love God with all your heart, soul, strength, and mind.**

   That means God comes first. Loving people without loving God first can turn into "people-pleasing." But loving God helps you love people in the right way.

2. **Love your neighbor as yourself.**

   "As yourself" means you care about your own needs. You want food, safety, respect, friends, and peace. Loving your neighbor means you want those good things for others too.

It doesn't mean you always feel warm feelings. It means you choose love.

Who Is My Neighbor?

In Luke 10, right after this verse, Jesus tells the story of the Good Samaritan. That story teaches something clear:your neighbor is not only your best friend.

Your neighbor can be:

- ✠ someone different from you
- ✠ someone who annoys you
- ✠ someone left out
- ✠ someone who is hurting
- ✠ someone you wouldn't normally choose

Loving your neighbor is not about "only loving my group." It's about loving like God loves.

What Love Looks Like (Not Just Words)

Real love is not just saying, "I love people."

Love looks like:

- ✠ including someone
- ✠ sharing
- ✠ listening
- ✠ helping when it costs you time
- ✠ speaking kindly
- ✠ telling the truth
- ✠ forgiving
- ✠ standing up for someone being mistreated

Love is often simple and practical.

Loving Your Neighbor Doesn't Mean You Have No Boundaries

Love is not the same as letting someone treat you badly. If someone is unsafe or cruel, you should tell a trusted adult.

You can still love someone by:

- ✟ praying for them
- ✟ refusing revenge
- ✟ asking for help
- ✟ keeping wise distance when needed

Love can be kind and wise at the same time.

Why This Matters

Loving your neighbor shows what you believe about God.

When you love people, you are showing:

- ✟ God's kindness
- ✟ God's patience
- ✟ God's truth
- ✟ God's mercy

Jesus loved His neighbors perfectly. He didn't ignore hurting people. He didn't treat people like objects. He loved with action.

Tiny Step to Try This Week

Choose one neighbor-love action every day this week:

- ✟ invite someone in
- ✟ help without being asked
- ✟ say one encouraging sentence
- ✟ share something
- ✟ pray for someone by name

WORKBOOK ACTIVITIES

1) Verse Copy (Handwriting Practice)

Copy the Bible focus verse:

"He answered, "'Love the Lord your God with all your heart and with all your soul and with all your strength and with all your mind'; and, 'Love your neighbor as yourself.'" - **Luke 10:27**

Copy it one more time:

____

____

____

____

2) Fill in the Blanks

"Love your _______________________ as _________________."

Write the missing words: _______________________________

3) True or False

Circle **True** or **False**.

1. My neighbor only means people who live near my house.

    True / False

2. Loving my neighbor includes actions, not only words.

    True / False

3. Loving my neighbor means I must let people harm me.

    True / False

4. Loving God helps me love people the right way.

    True / False

4) Neighbor List

Write 6 "neighbors" in your life (people around you):

1. ____

2. ____

3. ____

4. ____

5. ____

6. ____

Circle one person you can show love to this week.

5) Love Choices (Circle the Best One)

1. Someone is sitting alone.

    A) ignore them

    B) invite them to join

2. A classmate drops their books.

    A) walk by

    B) help pick them up

3. Someone is being teased.

    A) laugh along

    B) get help or stand with them

4. You feel annoyed at a sibling.

    A) be cruel

    B) use patient words

6) "As Yourself" Check

Write 3 things you want for yourself:

1. ____

2. ____

3. ____

Now write how you can want the same for others:

1. I can show _______________________________________

   by____ .

2. I can show _______________________________________

   by____ .

3. I can show _______________________________________

   by____ .

7) Neighbor Love Plan

Write one neighbor-love action you will do:

This week I will love my neighbor by ________________________

____

Write when you will do it: ____________________________

8) Prayer Practice

Write a prayer (6–10 lines):

"God, help me love You with my whole heart.

____

____

Help me love my neighbor as myself.

____

____

Show me who needs love today.

____

____

Help me take action with kindness and wisdom.

____

____

Amen."

9) **Knowledge Check (One-Minute Review)**

Answer in one short sentence:

What does Luke 10:27 teach you to do?

____

____

____

Love Your Neighbor BINGO!

INVITE SOMEONE TO PLAY	SAY SOMETHING ENCOURAGING	HELP CLEAN UP	SHARE SUPPLIES
HOLD THE DOOR	SIT WITH SOMEONE NEW	PRAY FOR A FRIEND	PICK UP TRASH
HELP A SIBLING	TELL THE TRUTH KINDLY	FORGIVE	OFFER A KIND SMILE
LET SOMEONE GO FIRST	SAY THANK YOU KINDLY	SHOW KINDNESS TO A NEIGHBOR	HELP SOMEONE CARRY SOMETHING

INSTRUCTIONS: • DO AN ACTION. MARK THE SQUARE.
• TRY TO GET 4 IN A ROW THIS WEEK.

WEEK 43
Be Brave in Hard Times

"Consider it pure joy, my brothers and sisters, whenever you face trials of many kinds, because you know that the testing of your faith produces perseverance." - James 1:2-3

BIG TRUTH: God can use hard times to grow your faith and strengthen your character.

WARM-UP: Have you ever had a hard week?

Hard times for kids can look like:

- a friendship problem
- a tough test
- being left out
- getting teased
- family stress
- feeling sick
- feeling sad for reasons you can't explain

When something hurts, it's normal to wish it would disappear fast.

James 1:2-3 doesn't pretend trials feel fun. But it teaches that God can use trials for good.

What James 1:2-3 Is Saying

James says, "Consider it pure joy, my brothers and sisters, whenever you face trials of many kinds, because you know that the testing of your faith produces perseverance."

That doesn't mean you have to smile about pain. It means you can choose a deeper joy because you trust God's purpose.

Then it explains why: "the testing of your faith produces steadfastness."

    ✞ **Testing** means your faith is being tried, like metal being tested to see if it's strong.

    ✞ **Steadfastness** means endurance, staying strong, not giving up.

Trials can be like exercise for your faith. Exercise can be hard and tiring, but it builds strength over time.

What Is a Trial?

A trial is something hard that tests you.

A trial can be:

    ✞ a difficult situation you can't control

    ✞ a problem that makes you feel weak

    ✞ a challenge that lasts longer than you want

Trials are not always punishment. Sometimes they are simply part of living in a broken world. But God can still use them.

How God Uses Hard Times

God can use trials to grow you in ways that comfort can't.

Hard times can:

    ✞ teach you to pray more honestly

    ✞ teach you to trust God instead of yourself

    ✞ help you grow patience

    ✞ help you learn compassion for others

    ✞ help you see what really matters

    ✞ help you practice endurance

God doesn't waste pain. That doesn't mean pain is good. It means God is good even in pain.

Joy in TrialsWhat It Really Means

Joy in trials means:

   ✝ "This hurts, but God is still with me."

   ✝ "This is hard, but God can help me endure."

   ✝ "I don't know how this will end, but I trust God."

Joy is not pretending. Joy is trusting.

What To Do When You're in a Trial

Here are four helpful steps:

1. **Tell God the truth.**

   You don't need fancy words:"God, this is hard."

2. **Ask for help.**

   Ask for strength, wisdom, and peace.

3. **Do the next right thing.**

   One step at a time. You don't have to solve everything today.

4. **Talk to a trusted person.**

   Parents, a pastor, a teacher, or a wise adult can help you.

You were not made to carry trials alone.

Tiny Step to Try This Week

When something hard happens, practice this sentence:

"God, help me endure and trust You."

WORKBOOK ACTIVITIES

1) Verse Copy (Handwriting Practice)

Copy the Bible focus phrase:

"Consider it pure joy, my brothers and sisters, whenever you face trials of many kinds, because you know that the testing of your faith produces perseverance." - **James 1:3**

Copy it one more time:

____

____

____

2) Fill in the Blanks

"The testing of your _________________ produces ____________."

Word bank: faith, perseverance

3) True or False

Circle **True** or **False**.

1. Trials are always easy and fun.   **True / False**

2. God can use trials to grow steadfastness.   **True / False**

3. Joy in trials means pretending you aren't hurting. **True / False**

4. I can ask God for help in hard times.   **True / False**

4) Big Word Helper (Match It)

Draw lines to match.

1. Trial   A) staying strong and not giving up

2. Testing   B) something hard that challenges you

3. Steadfastness   C) proving faith is real and growing it

5) My Trials List (Pick One)

Circle one that can be a trial for kids:

- ✧ a friend problem
- ✧ a hard test
- ✧ being teased
- ✧ family stress
- ✧ feeling sick
- ✧ feeling lonely

Now write one trial you're facing (or have faced):

____

____

6) Next Right Step

Write one "next right step" you can take in that trial:

My next right step is

____

____

____

7) Encourage Yourself with Truth

Finish the sentences:

✝ "God is with me when________________________ ."

✝ "God can help me endure by ________________ ."

✝ "I can ask for help from _________________ ."

8) Joy and Trust Practice

Circle the best response:

When I face a trial, I should:

A) give up and stop caring

B) tell God the truth and keep trusting

C) pretend it doesn't matter

Write one sentence of trust:

"Even when ________________________ , I will trust God."

9) Prayer Practice

Write a prayer (7–12 lines):

"God, this trial is hard.

____

____

Please help me endure.

____

____

Please give me wisdom for what to do next.

____

____

Help me not give up.

____

Thank You that You can grow my faith.

____

____

____

____

Amen."

10) Knowledge Check (One-Minute Review)

Answer in one short sentence:

What does James 1:2–3 teach about why trials matter?

____

____

____

God Helps Me Endure!
James 1:2–3
Rest
My step: ____________
Read God's Word
Tell the truth
My step: ____________
Don't quit
Take one step
Pray
My step: ____________

WEEK 44
Choose Humility

"Do nothing out of selfish ambition or vain conceit. Rather, in humility value others above yourselves," - Philippians 2:3

BIG TRUTH: **Humility means you don't make life all about you. You choose to honor others and serve like Jesus.**

WARM-UP: **HAVE YOU** ever wanted to be first, best, or noticed?

That's normal. People like praise. People like winning. People like being picked.

But the Bible warns us about two attitudes that can grow in our hearts:

✝ **selfish ambition** (I must win, even if I hurt others)

✝ **conceit** (I think I'm better than other people)

Philippians 2:3 teaches a better way:humility.

What Philippians 2:3 Is Saying

This verse gives two commands:

1. **"Do nothing from selfish ambition or conceit."**

   This doesn't mean you can't work hard or enjoy doing well. It means your goal shouldn't be "I matter most."

2. **"In humility count others more significant than yourselves."**

   This means you treat other people as valuable. You don't treat them like stepping stones.

Humility doesn't mean you hate yourself. Humility means you don't worship yourself.

Humility Is Not "Thinking You're the Worst"

Some kids think humility means saying, "I'm terrible," even when it's not true.

That's not humility. That's another kind of self-focus.

Real humility sounds like:

- ✟ "God gave me gifts, and I want to use them to help."
- ✟ "I can learn from others."
- ✟ "I can admit when I'm wrong."
- ✟ "I don't have to be the center."

Humility is honest. It's not fake.

Jesus Is the Best Example

Right after Philippians 2:3, the Bible talks about Jesus' humility.

Jesus is God's Son, but He came as a servant. He obeyed the Father. He cared for people. He gave His life.

That means humility is not weakness. Humility is strength used for love.

What Humility Looks Like at Home and School

Humility can show up in ordinary moments:

- ✟ letting someone else go first
- ✟ listening instead of interrupting
- ✟ sharing credit
- ✟ congratulating someone who did well
- ✟ saying "I was wrong"
- ✟ helping without needing attention
- ✟ choosing kindness when you could show off

Humility is a choice you make again and again.

What Pride Does

Pride often brings:

- ✝ arguments
- ✝ jealousy
- ✝ teasing
- ✝ pushing others down
- ✝ refusing correction
- ✝ refusing to apologize

Humility makes room for peace.

A Simple Humility Plan

When you walk into a room, ask:

- ✝ "Who can I encourage?"
- ✝ "Who needs help?"
- ✝ "How can I serve?"

That's not pretending you don't matter. It's choosing to love.

Tiny Step to Try This Week

Choose one humble action each day:

- ✝ say "good job" to someone else
- ✝ let someone else pick
- ✝ apologize quickly
- ✝ do a quiet act of service
- ✝ Then thank God for helping you.

WORKBOOK ACTIVITIES

1) Verse Copy (Handwriting Practice)

Copy the Bible focus verse:

"Do nothing out of selfish ambition or vain conceit. Rather, in humility value others above yourselves," - **Philippians 2:3**

Copy it one more time:

____

____

____

____

2) Fill in the Blanks

"Do nothing out of selfish ambition... Rather, in _______________

value others _________________ yourselves."

Word bank: humility, above

3) True or False

Circle **True** or **False**.

1. Humility means I hate myself.   **True / False**
2. Humility means I treat others as valuable.   **True / False**
3. Conceit means thinking I'm better than everyone.   **True / False**
4. Jesus showed humility by serving.   **True / False**

4) Humble or Proud? (Circle One)

1. You say, "I was wrong. I'm sorry."   **Humble / Proud**
2. You brag and put others down.   **Humble / Proud**
3. You let someone else go first.   **Humble / Proud**
4. You refuse to listen to correction.   **Humble / Proud**
5. You share credit on a group project.   **Humble / Proud**

5) Choose the Humble Response (Circle the Best Choice)

1. Your friend wins a game.

   A) get jealous and pout

   B) congratulate them

2. You get praised in class.

   A) brag

   B) say thank you and stay kind

3. Someone corrects you.

   A) argue

   B) listen and learn

4. A sibling needs help.

   A) ignore them

   B) help without complaining

6) My Humility Plan

Write one situation where you can choose humility this week:

Situation:____

____

Write one humble action you can take:

____

____

Finish this sentence:

"Humility looks like__________________________________ ."

7) Encourage Others

Write three encouraging sentences you could say:

1. ____

2. ____

3. ____

Write a prayer (6–10 lines):

"God, please help me choose humility.

____

____

Forgive me for selfish ambition and pride.

____

____

Help me count others as valuable.

____

____

Help me serve like Jesus today at ________________________

____

____

Amen."

9) **Knowledge Check (One-Minute Review)**

Answer in one short sentence:

What does Philippians 2:3 teach you to choose?

____

____

____

Choose Humility!

Finish Speech Bubbles with Humble Words

Philippians 2:3

WEEK 45
Tell the Truth

"The Lord detests lying lips, but he delights in people who are trustworthy." - Proverbs 12:22

BIG TRUTH: God loves truth. Telling the truth builds trust and honors God.

WARM-UP: Have you ever lied because you felt scared? Maybe you wanted to avoid trouble, avoid embarrassment, or look "better."

Lying can feel like a quick fix. But lies usually make the problem bigger.

What Proverbs 12:22 Is Saying

This verse teaches two strong things:

1. **God hates lies.**

   "Detests" means God strongly dislikes lying because lies hurt people.

2. **God loves trustworthiness.**

   God "delights" in people who are trustworthy—people whose words can be trusted.

Why Lies Hurt

Lies can:

✝ break friendships

✝ create confusion

✝ make adults stop trusting you

✝ make your heart feel heavy

Why Truth Is Brave

Truth can feel scary, but it is strong.

Telling the truth often leads to:

- ✠ forgiveness
- ✠ help
- ✠ peace
- ✠ real trust

A Simple Truth Plan

When you're tempted to lie, pause and ask:

- ✠ "What is the true story?"
- ✠ "What would I want someone to tell me?"
- ✠ "Can I ask God for courage?"

Tiny Step to Try This Week

Tell the truth quickly one time you would normally hide it. Then pray: "God, help me love truth."

WORKBOOK ACTIVITIES

1) Verse Copy (Handwriting Practice)

Copy the Bible focus verse:

"The Lord detests lying lips, but he delights in people who are trustworthy." - **Proverbs 12:22**

Copy it one more time:

____

____

2) Fill in the Blanks

"The Lord detests _____________ lips, but he delights in people who are ________________."

Word bank: lying, trustworthy

3) True or False

1. God loves it when I lie to stay out of trouble.   **True / False**

2. Truth builds trust.   **True / False**

3. A lie usually makes problems smaller.   **True / False**

4. God delights in trustworthy people.   **True / False**

4) What Kind of Lie? (Match It)

Draw lines to match.

1. "It wasn't me"   A) blame-shift lie

2. "I don't know" (but you do)   B) hide-it lie

3. "Everyone did it" (but they didn't)   C) exaggeration lie

5) Truth Choices (Circle the Best One)

1. You broke a rule.

    A) hide it
    B) tell the truth and ask forgiveness

2. You forgot homework.

    A) make up a story
    B) tell the truth and ask for help

3. A friend asks, "Did you talk about me?" and you did.

    A) deny it
    B) tell the truth and make it right

6) The Trust Builder

Write 3 ways truth builds trust:

1. ____

2. ____

3. ____

7) **Fix-It Steps (Write It)**

Finish the sentences:

    ✠ When I lie, I should____ .

    ✠ I can confess to____ .

    ✠ I can try to make it right by _______________________________ .

8) **Prayer Practice (6–10 lines)**

"God, You love truth.

____

____

Please forgive me for times I have lied.

____

____

Help me be brave and honest, even when it's hard.

____

____

Help me be trustworthy at _______________________________________

____

____

Amen."

9) **Knowledge Check (One-Minute Review)**

In one sentence: What does Proverbs 12:22 teach about truth?

____

____

____

Tell the Truth!

Proverbs 12:22

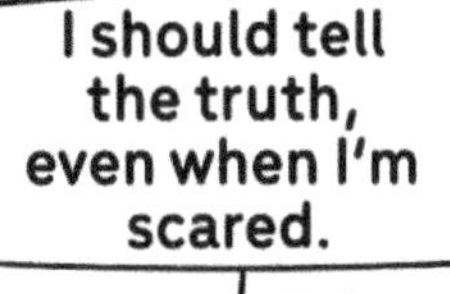

I should tell the truth, even when I'm scared.

| True | False |

It is okay to hide the truth.

| True | False |

God wants me to tell the truth.

| True | False |

Confession is a brave step.

| True | False |

God delights in trustworthy people.

| True | False |

Blaming others is the right thing to do.

| True | False |

Lying is okay if it helps me.

| True | False |

Honesty pleases God.

| True | False |

Telling the truth shows courage.

| True | False |

A small lie doesn't matter.

| True | False |

I can lie to avoid trouble.

| True | False |

Instructions: *Read each box. Circle True if it is right. Circle False if it is wrong. Then draw a line to the Truth Filter or the Trash.*

WEEK 46
Give Generously

"Each of you should give what you have decided in your heart to give, not reluctantly or under compulsion, for God loves a cheerful giver."
- 2 Corinthians 9:7

BIG TRUTH: God wants His people to give with joy, because He first gave to us.

WARM-UP: Have you ever shared something you really wanted to keep? Sharing can feel hard. But generous giving is one way we show love.

What 2 Corinthians 9:7 Is Saying

This verse teaches:

- **Give on purpose** ("decided in your heart")
- **Don't give with complaining** ("not reluctantly")
- **Don't give because someone forced you** ("not under compulsion")
- **Give with joy** ("cheerful giver")

What Can Kids Give?

Giving isn't only money. Kids can give:

- time
- kindness
- help
- sharing supplies
- encouraging words
- saving a small amount to bless someone

Tiny Step to Try This Week

Pick **one giving idea** and do it with a cheerful heart.

WORKBOOK ACTIVITIES

1) Verse Copy

Copy 2 Corinthians 9:7 (or the first sentence). Copy again.

____

____

____

____

2) **Fill in the Blanks**

"God loves a ______________________________________ giver."

Word bank:cheerful

3) **True or False**

1. Giving only counts if I give a lot.   **True / False**

2. God cares about my heart when I give.   **True / False**

3. It's okay to give while complaining the whole time.   **True / False**

4. Giving can include time and kindness.   **True / False**

4) **Give What? (Circle All That Count)**

money / time / kindness / help / teasing /

sharing / encouragement / ignoring

5) **Cheerful or Grumpy? (Circle One)**

1. "Fine, take it."   **Cheerful / Grumpy**

2. "I'm glad to help."   **Cheerful / Grumpy**

3. "I guess I have to."   **Cheerful / Grumpy**

4. "Here, this is for you."   **Cheerful / Grumpy**

6) Spot a Need (Write 3 Needs You Notice)

____

____

____

7) My Giving Plan (Make It Real)

This week I will give __________ by _______________________

on (day/time) _________________________.

8) Thank God for Giving

Write 3 gifts God has given you:

____

____

____

9) Prayer Practice

"God, thank You for giving to me.

____

____

____

Help me give with joy.

____

____

Show me one person I can bless this week.

____

____

Amen."

 Knowledge Check

What kind of giver does God love?

____

____

____

My one giving plan this week: ______________

WEEK 47
Obey God at Home

"As for me and my household, we will serve the Lord." - Joshua 24:15

BIG TRUTH: God wants families to choose His ways at home, together.

WARM-UP: Home is where your habits grow. Sometimes it's easier to act kind at school than at home. But God cares about both.

What Joshua 24:15 Is Saying

Joshua was a leader. He told the people they had to choose:

✟ follow idols, or

✟ **serve the Lord**

Joshua said, "My house will serve the Lord." That means: "In our home, we choose God's ways."

What Serving God Looks Like at Home

Serving God at home can look like:

✟ obeying parents with respect

✟ telling the truth

✟ doing chores without arguing

✟ using calm words

✟ praying together

✟ forgiving quickly

Tiny Step to Try This Week

Choose **one "serve the Lord" habit** to practice at home all week.

WORKBOOK ACTIVITIES

1) Verse Copy

Copy Joshua 24:15 (short version). Copy again.

____

____

____

2) Fill in the Missing Words

"As for me and my _____________, we will _____________ the Lord."

Word bank:household, serve

3) True or False

1. God only cares about how I act at church.   **True / False**

2. Serving God includes how I treat my family.   **True / False**

3. Obeying with a bad attitude is the same as
    obeying with a good attitude.   **True / False**

4. Families can serve God together.   **True / False**

4) Home Choices (Circle the Best One)

1. Parent asks you to do a chore.

    A) argue

    B) obey and do your best

2. Sibling annoys you.

    A) insult them

    B) use calm words or walk away

3. You made a mess.

    A) hide it

    B) tell the truth and clean it

5) Serve the Lord at Home (Write 6 Actions)

____

____

____

6) Family Action List (Pick 3)

Circle 3: pray / read one verse / help with chores / kind words / forgive / complain less / encourage / listen

7) My "Serve the Lord" Plan

This week, I will serve the Lord at home by

____

____

____

8) Prayer Practice

"God, help our home serve You.

____

____

Help me obey with respect and love.

____

____

____

Help me do my part today.

Amen."

9) Knowledge Check

What does Joshua 24:15 say Joshua chose for his household?

____

____

____

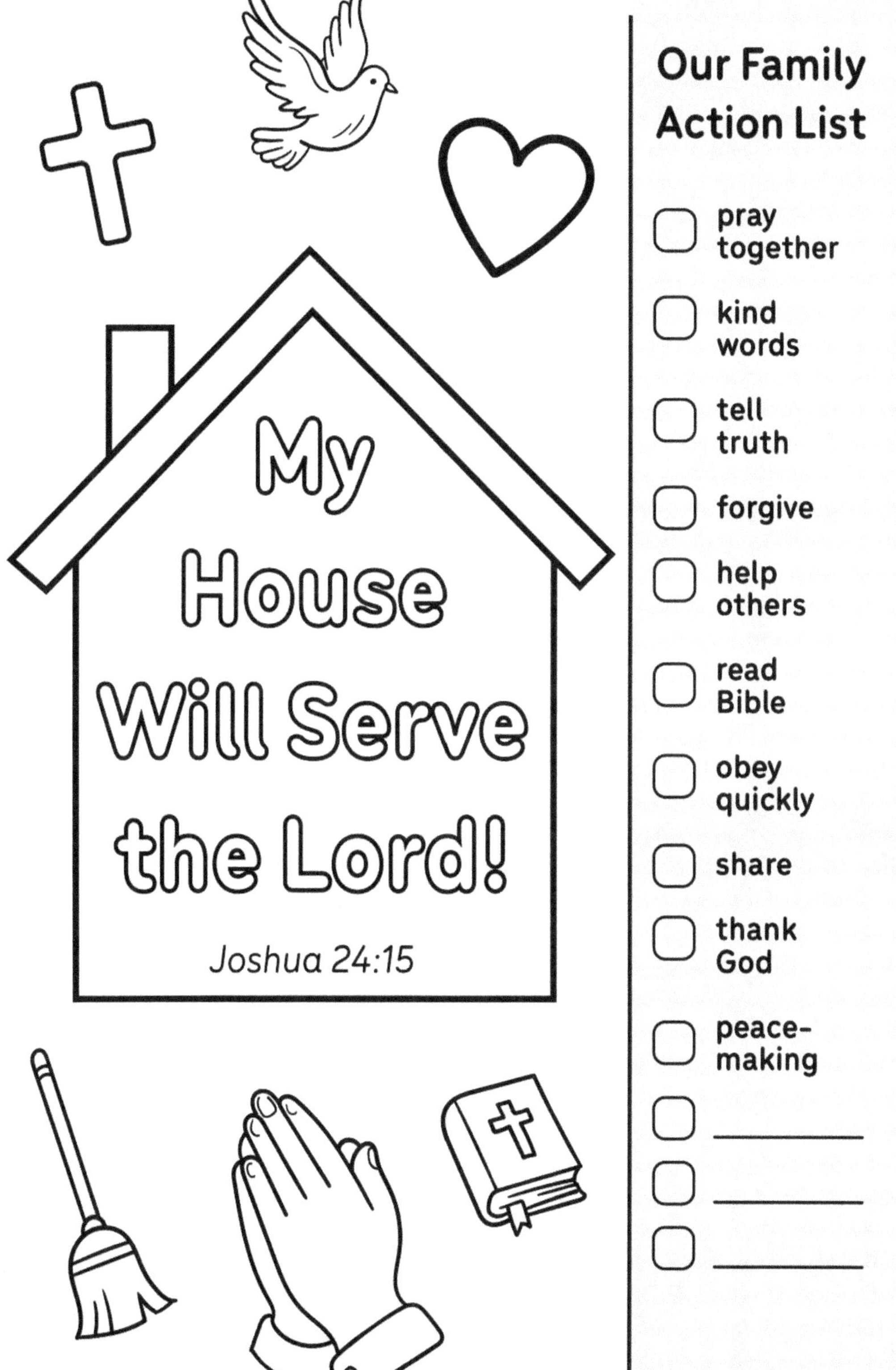
My House Will Serve the Lord!
Joshua 24:15
Our Family Action List
pray together
kind words
tell truth
forgive
help others
read Bible
obey quickly
share
thank God
peace-making

WEEK 48
Shine Your Light

"Let your light shine before others, that they may see your good deeds and glorify your Father in heaven." - Matthew 5:16

BIG TRUTH: God uses your good deeds to point people to Him.

WARM-UP: Have you ever been in a dark room when someone turned on a light? Light makes it easier to see and feel safe.

What Matthew 5:16 Is Saying

Jesus says your life can be like light. When people see your kindness, honesty, and love, they can think: "God must be good."

This verse is not saying, "Show off." It's saying, "Do good so God gets glory."

What Light Looks Like

Light actions can be:

- ✝ include someone left out
- ✝ help without being asked
- ✝ speak gently
- ✝ tell the truth
- ✝ forgive
- ✝ pray for someone
- ✝ share

Tiny Step to Try This Week

Do one "light action" quietly each day.

WORKBOOK ACTIVITIES

1) Verse Copy

Copy Matthew 5:16. Copy again.

____

____

____

____

____

2) Fill in the Blanks

"Let your ___________________ shine before others... so they may glorify your ___________ in heaven."

Word bank: light, Father

3) True or False

1. Shining my light means bragging.   True / False
2. Good deeds can point people to God.   True / False
3. I can shine my light at school and at home.   True / False
4. God wants people to glorify Him.   True / False

4) Light or Not Light? (Circle One)

1. Encourage someone who failed.   Light / Not light
2. Tease someone to look cool.   Light / Not light
3. Share supplies.   Light / Not light
4. Gossip.   Light / Not light
5. Help clean up.   Light / Not light

5) Why Do We Shine? (Circle One)

A) so people praise me

B) so people glorify God

6) My 10 "Light Actions" List

Write 10 ways you can shine God's light this week:

____

____

____

____

____

____

____

____

7) Who Needs Light?

Write 3 people you can bless:

____

____

____

8) Prayer Practice

"Father, help my light shine.

Help me do good with a humble heart.

Let people see You through my actions.

Amen."

9) Knowledge Check

What does Matthew 5:16 say people should do when they see your good deeds?

____

____

____

Shine Your Light!
Matthew 5:16
Light action 1:
Light action 1:
Light action 1:
Light action 1:
Light action 1:
Light action 1:
Light action 1:
Light action 1:
Light action 1:
Light action 1:

PART NINE
Angels, Spiritual Battle, and the Future

WEEK 49
Remember God Sends Angels

"Are not all angels ministering spirits sent to serve those who will inherit salvation?" - Hebrews 1:14

BIG TRUTH: God sends angels to serve His plans and help His people.

WARM-UP: Angels can feel mysterious. Movies sometimes make up strange ideas. So we stick to what the Bible truly says.

What Hebrews 1:14 Is Saying

This verse teaches:

- ✝ Angels are **real** spiritual beings God made.
- ✝ Angels are **servants**, not gods.
- ✝ Angels do what **God sends** them to do.
- ✝ God uses angels to help His people, according to His wise plan.

What We Should Remember

- ✝ We worship **God**, not angels.
- ✝ Angels obey God.
- ✝ God is the one who protects, leads, and saves.

Tiny Step to Try This Week

When you feel afraid, pray:

"God, thank You that You help me. Please guard my heart and guide me."

WORKBOOK ACTIVITIES

1) Verse Copy

Copy Hebrews 1:14 (or the first half). Copy again.

____

____

2) Fill in the Blanks

"Angels are ministering spirits sent to ___________ those who will inherit ___________."

Word bank: serve, salvation

3) True or False

1. Angels are made-up stories.   **True / False**
2. Angels serve God's plans.   **True / False**
3. We should worship angels.   **True / False**
4. God cares for His people.   **True / False**

4) Who Does What? (Circle the Right One)

1. Who saves us?   **God / Angels**
2. Who should we worship?   **God / Angels**
3. Who sends angels?   **God / People**

5) Bible Job Match (Draw Lines)

Match the angel job to the meaning:

1. messenger   A) brings a message
2. servant   B) helps carry out God's will
3. protector (by God's command)   C) helps keep safe

6) "God Helps Me" Matching

Match the feeling to a faith response (draw lines):

✢ afraid →   "I can pray."

✢ lonely →   "God is with me."

✢ tempted →   "God can help me choose right."

✢ worried →   "God is wise and cares."

✢ sad →   "God comforts."

7) Thank God for Help (Write 3)

1. God helps me when _______________________________________

2. God helps me by____

3. I can ask God for help about_____________________________

8) Prayer Practice

"God, thank You that You are Lord over everything.

Thank You for helping Your people.

Help me trust You when I feel_________________________________ .

Amen."

9) Knowledge Check

In one sentence: What does Hebrews 1:14 teach about angels?

____

____

____

____

God Sends Help!

Hebrews 1:14

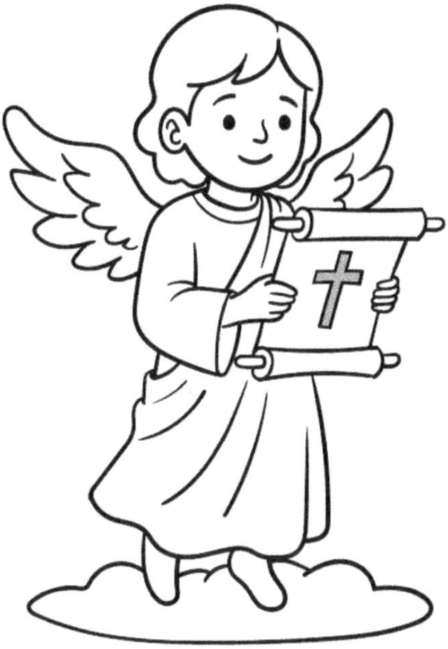

God Helps Me

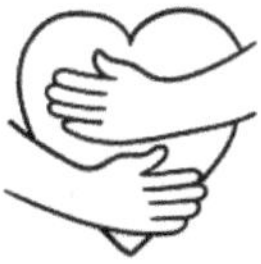

Comfort ○ ○

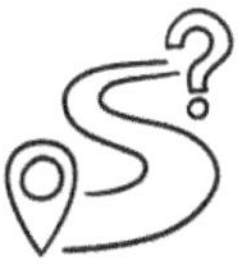

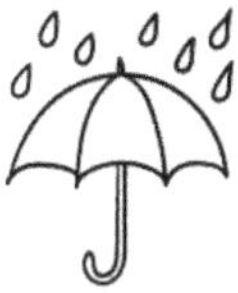

Protection ○ ○

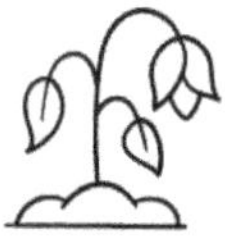

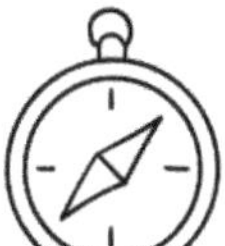

Guidance ○ ○

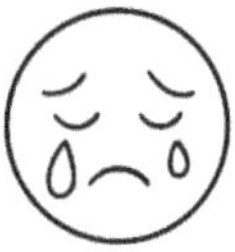

Reminder ○ ○

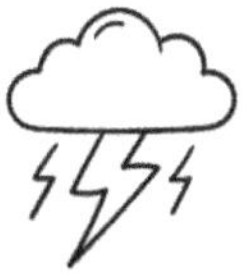

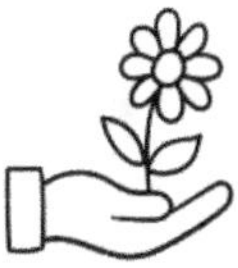

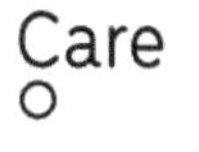

Care ○ ○

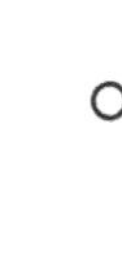

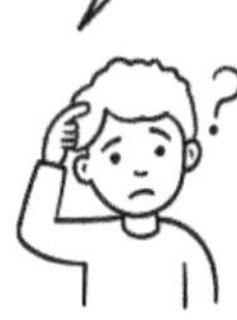

WEEK 50
Put On God's Armor

"Put on the full armor of God, so that you can take your stand against the devil's schemes." - Ephesians 6:11

BIG TRUTH: God gives His people spiritual armor so we can stand strong against lies and temptation.

WARM-UP: Have you ever felt pulled to do wrong? That pull can come from inside (sinful desires) and outside (temptation and lies).

What Ephesians 6:11 Is Saying

This verse teaches:

- There is a real spiritual battle.
- The devil uses "schemes" (tricks and lies).
- God doesn't leave us unprotected.
- We must **put on** God's armor (choose it on purpose).

What "Armor" Means (Kid Version)

God's armor is not metal. It's God's truth helping you:

- believe what's true
- choose what's right
- trust God when you're scared
- resist temptation

Tiny Step to Try This Week

When you face temptation, say: "God, help me stand strong."

1) Verse Copy

Copy Ephesians 6:11. Copy again.

____

____

____

____

2) Fill in the Blanks

"Put on the full ______________ of God..."

3) True or False

1.	God wants me to stand strong.	**True / False**
2.	The devil never lies.	**True / False**
3.	God gives help for spiritual battles.	**True / False**
4.	Armor is something I "choose" to use.	**True / False**

4) Armor Match (Draw Lines)

1. Belt of truth
2. Breastplate of righteousness
3. Shield of faith
4. Helmet of salvation
5. Sword of the Spirit (Word of God)

A) helps me love honesty

B) helps protect my heart from sin

C) helps block lies

D) helps guard my mind with hope

E) helps me answer lies with Scripture

5) Spot the Lie (Write L or T)

1. "No one will know."

2. "God can help me obey."

3. "I can't change."

4. "Jesus forgives when I confess."

5. "Revenge will fix it."

6) My Armor Plan

Write one way you will use:

✝ truth this week

____

____

✝ faith this week

____

____

✝ God's Word this week

____

____

7) Prayer Practice

"God, help me put on Your armor.

Help me stand against lies and temptation.

Help me choose what is right today.

Amen."

8) Knowledge Check

Why does God tell you to put on the armor?

____

____

____

Put On God's Armor!

Ephesians 6:11

One lie I will fight with truth: _______________

____

WEEK 51
Hope in Jesus' Return

"For the Lord himself will come down from heaven... and so we will be with the Lord forever." - 1 Thessalonians 4:16–17 (kid-friendly summary)

BIG TRUTH: Jesus will return, and God's people will be with Him forever. That gives real hope.

WARM-UP: **HAVE YOU** ever waited for someone you love to come back—like a parent from a trip?

Waiting can feel long. Hope helps you wait.

What This Passage Teaches

The Bible teaches:

- ✝ Jesus will truly return.

- ✝ God keeps His promises.

- ✝ Believers will be with Jesus forever.

- ✝ This hope comforts us when we feel sad or scared.

Hope Is Not Wishful Thinking

Bible hope is not "maybe." Bible hope is strong trust in God's promise.

Tiny Step to Try This Week

When you feel worried, say: "Jesus, You are King. You will keep Your promises."

WORKBOOK ACTIVITIES

1) Verse Copy

Copy the phrase:"We will be with the Lord forever." Copy again.

____

____

2) Fill in the Blanks

"Jesus will _____________, and we will be with the Lord _____________."

Word bank:return, forever

3) True or False

1. Jesus might come back, but we can't really know.   **True / False**

2. Bible hope is trusting God's promises.   **True / False**

3. Jesus' return can comfort God's people.   **True / False**

4. Being with Jesus forever is good news.   **True / False**

4) Hope vs. Worry (Circle One)

1. "God forgot me."   **Hope / Worry**

2. "Jesus keeps promises."   **Hope / Worry**

3. "Nothing will ever get better."   **Hope / Worry**

4. "God will make all things right."   **Hope / Worry**

5) Comfort Words (Write 3)

Write 3 hope sentences you can say when you feel sad:

____

____

____

6) Promise Stars (Write 5 Promises of Hope)

(Short phrases—kid words)

____

____

____

____

7) Prayer Practice

"Jesus, thank You that You will return.

Help me wait with hope.

Help me live faithfully today.

Amen."

8) Knowledge Check

What is one reason Jesus' return gives you hope?

____

____

____

Watch and Hope!

Write a hope promise on each star.

1 Thessalonians 4:16–17

WEEK 52
Look Forward to New Creation

"He will wipe every tear from their eyes. There will be no more death or mourning or crying or pain..." — Revelation 21:4

BIG TRUTH: God will make everything new. Heaven and the new earth will be free from sadness and pain.

WARM-UP: Have you ever wished you could erase sadness like wiping a chalkboard clean? God promises something even better: a world made new.

What Revelation 21:4 Is Saying

God promises:

- ✝ He will wipe away tears.
- ✝ There will be **no more** death.
- ✝ No more mourning, crying, or pain.
- ✝ The old brokenness will be gone.

Why This Matters Now

Life is not always easy. People get sick. People die. Hearts break.

But God's future is bright, and Jesus guarantees it.

Tiny Step to Try This Week

Write one "new creation hope sentence" and say it when you feel sad.

WORKBOOK ACTIVITIES

1) Verse Copy

Copy Revelation 21:4 (or the first sentence). Copy again.

____

____

____

____

2) Fill in the Blanks

"He will wipe every ___________ from their eyes."

Word bank:tear

3) True or False

1. God promises a future with no more pain.　　**True / False**

2. God doesn't care about our tears.　　**True / False**

3. New creation means God will make things right.　　**True / False**

4. Revelation 21:4 is meant to give hope.　　**True / False**

4) "No More..." (Fill It In)

Write the missing words:

✝ No more _________________________________

✝ No more _________________________________

✝ No more _________________________________

✝ No more _________________________________

✝ (Word bankdeath, mourning, crying, pain)

5) Broken vs. New (Match It)

1. tears　　　　A) comfort

2. pain　　　　B) healing

3. death　　　　C) life

4. brokenness　　　　D) made new

6) Hope Picture (Draw + Caption)

Draw what you think "no more pain" could look like.

Caption: "God will make ________________________________ new."

7) Thank God for Future Hope (Write 3)

____

____

____

8) Prayer Practice

"God, thank You for Your promise of new creation.

Thank You that You will wipe away tears.

Help me trust You when life feels hard.

Amen."

9) Knowledge Check

What are two "no more" promises in Revelation 21:4?

____

____

____

God Makes All Things New!

Revelation 21:4

GLOSSARY
(Kid-Friendly Theology Words)

✟ **Angel** A spirit being God made to serve Him and carry out His plans.

✟ **Armor of God** God's help to stand strong against lies and temptation.

✟ **Cheerful giver** Someone who gives with joy, not complaining.

✟ **Confess** To tell the truth to God about sin and agree it is wrong.

✟ **Faith** Trusting God and His promises, even when you can't see everything.

✟ **Forgive** To let go of revenge and choose love instead.

✟ **Gospel** The good news that Jesus saves sinners.

✟ **Grace** God's kindness gift that we don't earn.

✟ **Heaven** Being with God—perfect joy and peace.

✟ **Humility** Not making life all about yourself; treating others as valuable.

✟ **Hope (Bible hope)** Strong trust that God will keep His promises.

✟ **New creation** God's future world made new—no more pain or sadness.

✟ **Obey** To do what God says because you trust Him.

✟ **Pride** Acting like you are the most important or better than others.

✟ **Salvation** God rescuing us from sin and bringing us into His family.

✟ **Temptation** Pressure to sin—wanting to do what God says is wrong.

✟ **Truth** What matches God's Word and God's character.

✟ **Trustworthy** Someone whose words and actions can be trusted.

✟ **Worship** Loving God most and honoring Him as King.

CERTIFICATE OF COMPLETION

52 Weeks of Systematic Theology Workbook for Kids

This certificate is awarded to:

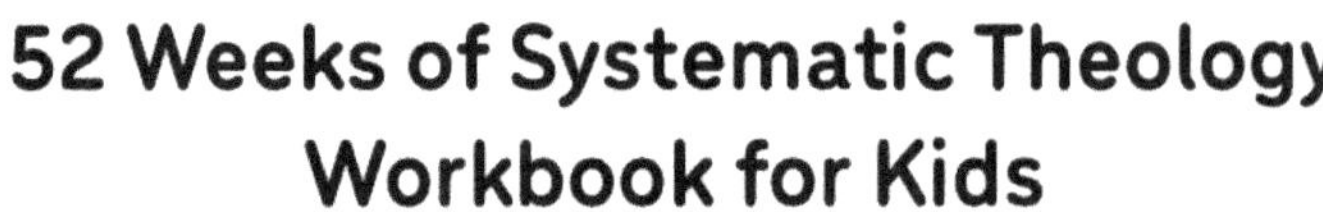

Name: ________________________________

for faithfully completing:

52 Weeks of Learning God's Big Truths

through reading, writing, and activities
in God's Word.

Date: ____________________

Parent / Grown-Up Signature:

____

One truth I want to remember most:

____

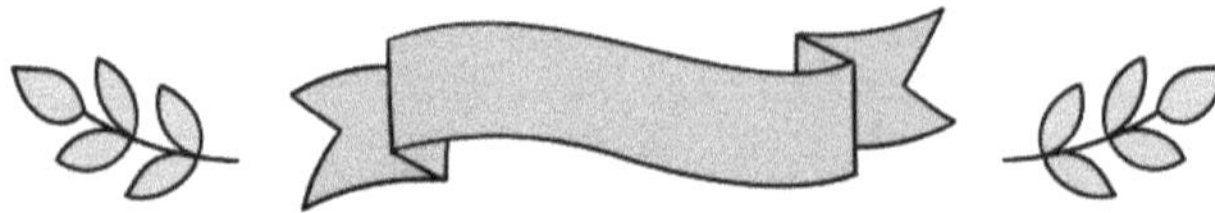

Check out another book in the series

Welcome Aboard, Check Out This Limited-Time Free Bonus!

Ahoy, reader! Welcome to the Ahoy Publications family, and thanks for snagging a copy of this book! Since you've chosen to join us on this journey, we'd like to offer you something special.

Check out the link below for a FREE e-book filled with delightful facts about American History.

But that's not all - you'll also have access to our exclusive email list with even more free e-books and insider knowledge. Well, what are ye waiting for? Click the link below to join and set sail toward exciting adventures in American History.

Access your bonus here

https://ahoypublications.com/

Or, Scan the QR code!